STOICISM

CONTENTS

Introduction
1. Understanding the principles and concepts of stoicism
2. The pillars of stoicism
3. Stoicism in the modern world
Afterword

INTRODUCTION

Stoicism is a branch of philosophy that is said to be created for people who live their lives in the real world. It is an extraordinary ancient philosophy that is designed to make sure that that we live our lives in more virtuous, happier, more resilient and wiser manner, which as a result makes us better individuals, better professionals, and better parents.

In simple words, the aim of Stoicism is to assist people in living the best life attainable to them. It is one of the philosophies of life that capitalizes on positive feelings or emotions, diminishes negative feelings or emotions and helps people in cultivating the virtues of their character. Stoicism provides a foundation for living a good life. It reminds people of the things that are of utmost importance, and providing real and pragmatic approaches to achieve more of valuable things.

The philosophies of Stoicism are learnt and practiced by politicians, entrepreneurs, athletes, artists, just to mention a few in today's world, and it is also known to be one of the famous thread through some of the great leaders in history. It has been put to use by presidents, kings, artists, entrepreneurs, and writers. Some of the notable people that were obviously influenced by stoicism include; Thomas Jefferson, George Washington, Adam Smith, General James Mattis, Theodore Roosevelt, John Stuart Mill, and so on. Stoicism was created with the intention of it being very useful, actionable, and understandable. It can be practiced without having to learn a completely new philosophical dictionary or engaging in rigorous meditation exercises. Instead, it provides a quick, beneficial, and pragmatic approach to find peace, and develop the strengths of one's character. These attributes and benefits of stoicism will be elaborated further in various chapters of this book.

The motivating factor for the study of stoicism in today's world is that stoic practices and thoughts are very prevalent in the modern age, and we often apply them in our daily lives.

DEFINITION OF STOICISM

Stoicism is known as a school of Hellenistic philosophy that was founded in Athens by Zeno of Citium in the third century. It emphasizes on the importance of nature as its most crucial element. Stoicism is a philosophy that is based on virtue ethics that produce happiness and well-being, which is informed by its logic systems, and its natural world view, stating that putting virtue into practice is both sufficient and necessary to achieve happiness and well-being (eudiamonia). This means that happiness and prosperity comes by living based on ethics. Stoicism derives its name from the painted porch called *Stoapoikile* which was where Zeno conducted lectures for his students.

Stoicism as a school of thought was very famous and thrived in the Greek and Roman ages. It was indeed a sublime and lofty philosophy in the history of the civilization of Western culture. In order to promote the influence of Stoicism on the affair of human beings, Stoics have continuously held on to the believe that the ultimate aim of all its processes is to formulate or generate a mode of conduct that is characterized by a peaceful mind and the assurance of moral values.

Stoicism is a philosophy of ancient times that was one of the most famous societal disciplines in the Western culture, practiced by people irrespective of their social class – whether rich or poor, powerful or weak, as they are all in pursuit of living a good life. The concept of Stoicism often appears new-fangled to people or misunderstood by the majority, except for those who have devoted themselves to search for knowledge. To an average individual, Stoicism appear to be an action-oriented, versatile, and life-changing way of living, which has become a way of achieving emotionlessness. In the correct sense, Stoicism serves as a tool used in the pursuit of things needed to live a great and good life, such as wisdom, perseverance, and self-mastery, rather than a mere field that can only be understood by few individuals. Many great minds in history fully understood and sought out the essence of stoicism. They studied, read, admired, or quoted the Stoics. The Stoics of ancient ages themselves were also well informed and competent. Names such as Marcus Aurelius, Epictetus, and Seneca are well identified with Stoicism. These great men of the past found a great deal in Stoicism, that it basically provides the needed wisdom, strength, and stamina for all challenges of life.

Stoics are majorly known for asserting that the only good for human beings is virtue, and other external things such as pleasure, health, and wealth are neither good nor bad in themselves, and that the value of such external things is in serving as materials upon which virtue acts. Stoicism forms one of the important foundational methods to virtue ethics.

Another assertion of the Stoics is that certain emotions that leads to destruction are as a result of errors in judgement, and that people should desire to maintain a will, which should be in accordance with nature. As a result of this, the Stoics believed that what best indicates a person's philosophy was not what is said by the person, but the behaviour of that person. The Stoics thought everything has its foundation in nature, and that one has to fully grasp the rules that guide the natural order in order to love a good life.

Epictetus and Seneca, and many other Stoics of the ancient age emphasized on the fact that the emotional resilience of a sage to misfortune is made possible because virtue is enough for happiness.

THE ORIGIN OF STOICISM

The origin of Stoicism can be traced back to 304 BC, when Zeno, a merchant got shipwrecked while on the course of trading. When he got to Anthens, he got the basic knowledge about philosophy by Crates, a Cynic philosopher, and Stilpo, a Megarian philosopher. This knowledge of philosophy caused a change in his life. Later, Zeno made a joke about his experience, and stated that "I made a prosperous voyage when is suffered shipwreck."

Stoicism was initially referred to as "Zenonism", a name derived from Zeno of Citrium, the founder. However, the name was only used within a period and dropped, which may be because the Stoics could not vouch for the perfect wisdom of their founders, and to prevent the risk of the Stoicism philosophies becoming an ordinary cult of personality. As mentioned earlier, the term "Stoicism" was derived from "*Stoa Poikile*", which literally means a "a painted porch". It was a place where Zeno of Citrium discussed ideas with the gathering of his followers. As a result of this Stoicism is sometimes referred to as "The porch" philosophy. The followers of Stoicism were firstly called Zenonians, but because of Zeno's commendable level of humility, the school of philosophy he founded did not carry his name ultimately, which is not a common attribute of schools in his days.

HISTORY OF STOICISM

As explained in the previous sections of this book on how Zeno taught philosophy at the *Stoa Poikile*, from which the name Stoicism was derived. Zeno decided to teach and discuss his philosophy with his students in a public place, known as Colonnade, which he chose above the *Agora*, a central point of meeting in Anthens.

The ideas of Zeno is formed from the Cynics' idea. The founding father of Cynics philosophy is Antisthenes, who has been Socrates' disciple. Chrysippus who was the most prominent follower of Zeno, was responsible for forming the phenomenon now known as Stocism. Roman Stoics who emerged later concentrated on promoting a life that is in concordance within the scope of the universe which no one has control over.

The history of Stoicism is often divided into three phases by scholars, which are:
- The Early Stoa – from the discoveries of Zeno to Antipater
- The Middle Stoa – which includes Posidonius and Panaetius
- The Late Stoa – which includes Seneca, Musonius Rufus, Marcus Arelius, and Epictetus.

It is important to note that works from the first and second phases of Stoicism did not survive, and only the Roman texts, which are products of the third phase (the late Stoa) survived. Stoicism emerged as the first most famous philosophy among the well informed elites in the Roman Empire and Hellenistic world, to the extent that Gilbert Murray stated that "all Alexander's successors have called themselves Stoics."

To broaden our understanding of Stoicism, there is the need to further elaborate on its history and metamorphosis, from the age of ancient Stoicism to the medieval and modern practice of Stoicism.

AN OVERVIEW OF PRECEDING PHILOSOPHIES

Stoicism is regarded as a Hellenistic eudaimonic philosophy, which implies that we can assume it to be influenced by its contemporaries and predecessors, in addition to being in open important communicate with them. These consists of Socratic thinking, because it has arrived to us specially through the early Platonic dialogues; Aristotelianism of the Peripatetic school; the Platonism of the Academic school, specifically in its Sceptical phase; Scepticism; Epicureanism; and Cynicism. It is really worth noting, in order to place matters into context, that a quantitative look at the extant statistics regarding recognized philosophers of the historical Greco-Roman world estimates that the main colleges of the time were: Academics-Platonists, Stoics, Epicureans, and Peripatetics-Aristotelians, listed in descending order.

The term eudaimonia refers to a life worth living, which is often translated in modern days as "happiness" in the broad sense, or more precisely, fullness or flourishing. To the Greco-Romans, this often implied - but was not necessarily entirely defined by - excellence in moral qualities. The idea is thus closely related to ethics, an approach most famously associated with Aristotle and his Nicomachian ethics, and revived by a number of philosophers in modern times, including Alasdair MacIntyre and Philippa Foot.

The concept of Stoicism is understood best within the context of the variations amongst a number of the similar faculties of the time. For instance, Socrates argued within the Euthydemus, that virtue, and especially the four cardinal virtues of courage, wisdom, temperance, and justice, are the only good virtues, and that everything else is neither right nor wrong, good or bad of and in itself. In contrast to this, Aristotle's list of twelve virtues had been vital but not enough for eudaimonia. One additionally needed a positive virtues, which include wealth, education, health, or even a piece of right looks. In different words, Aristotle expounded the alternatively common sense perception that a flourishing lifestyle is a component effort, due to the fact that an individual can actually and have to domesticate his or her character, and component luck, in the shape of the cultural and physical situations that have effects on and form one`s lifestyles. This can be contrasted with the alternatively extreme assertion of the Cynics, who like Socrates, did not think that the only good was virtue, but that the extra good virtues that Aristotle was concerned about had been truly distractions and had to be undoubtedly avoided. Cynics similar to Diogenes of Sinope had been well-known for their eclectic or rather shall we alternatively prefer ascetic lifestyles, as is epitomized with the aid of using a tale told by Diogenes Laertius.

The Aristotelian method or approach can be thought about in one way as being aristocratic a bit: if one is not opportune to have certain chances in life, one cannot gain eudaimonia. In contradiction to this, the Cynics have been preaching as a substitute, an extraordinarily minimalist way of life, that's difficult to exercise for majority of human beings. What the Stoics attempted to do was to create a balance at the centre, by applauding the dual important ideas, that virtue is the simplest actual good, in itself enough for eudaimonia irrespective of one's circumstances, also in addition to that, other things wealth, health, and education can be reasonably embraced or rejected, as in the cases of ignorance, poverty and sickness, so long as they are not confused for matters with inherent value.

STOICISM OF THE ANCIENT GREEK

The enormity of the life and concept of the Greek city-state (known as polis) ended with the demise of Aristotle in 322 BC and that of Alexander the Great in 323 BC. Athens pride of cultural superiority and civilization was passed on to different cities, such as Rome, Alexandria, and Pergamum, because of the loss of position as the World's centre of attraction. The Greek polis allowed bigger political units; local rule become changed to the use of remote governors. The previous difference among barbarian and the Greek became destroyed; provincial and tribal loyalties have been damaged apart, firstly by Alexander, then later by the Roman legions. The lack of freedom of the populace diminished the freeman concept and led to the performing of duties and rendering of services to the ruler, who has a moral force with little significance. The foremost civic and cosmic intimacy of order was now substituted with political and social disorder.

Stoicism started in a world that is experiencing significant changes, where the foremost ways of comprehension and codes of conducts are no longer applicable. The beliefs of older schools also have notable influence on Stoicism. The Milesians, who were the foremost Greek Philosophers called attention to nature's beauty and cosmic orders. Later on, the power of thoughts and reason was emphasized on by monist Parmenides of Elea, while the precursor of the philosophy of becoming, Heracleitus of Ephesus, had consented to the steadiness of change and that ability of divine fire to illuminate all things at everywhere. A deeper comprehension of human nature got here with Socrates, the philosopher, who exemplified sophia and sapientia ("wisdom" in Greek and Latin). Of the numerous faculties of philosophy originating from Socrates, the Megarian and Cynic faculties have been influential in the early improvement of Stoic doctrine. The Cynics laid emphasis on easy life, freed and unadorned from emotional engagements, and the Megarians conducted studies on paradoxes, dialectic, and logical form.

The "Greek" segment of the Stoa covers the primary and second periods, from the founding of the college through Zeno to the transferring of the middle of gravity from Athens to Rome in the time of Posidonius (I Century B.C.E.), who is a friend of Cicero—a non Stoic,, who is one of our great assets on early Stoicism. Stoicism became now no longer simply born, it thrived in Athens, irrespective of the fact that majority of its exponents are from the Eastern Mediterranea, they include: Zeno from Citium, which is in present day Cyprus, Chrysippus from Soli - present day Southern Turkey), and Cleanthes from Assos - present day Western Turkey, amongst others.

From inception, Stoicism was known to be a Socratic philosophy, and the Stoics themselves saw nothing wrong with this kind of label. Zeno commenced his research under the Cynic Crates, and Cynicism constantly had a robust effect on Stoicism, all of the manner to the writings of Epictetus that came later. But Zeno additionally counted amongst his instructors Polemo, the pinnacle of the Academy, and Stilpo, of the Megarian school which was founded by Euclid of Megaria, a student of Socrates. This is applicable due to the fact that Zeno intended to expatiate a philosophy that became each of Socratic inspiration and a compromise among Polemo`s and Stilpo`s assertions, because the former agreed with the concept that there are outside goods, even though they're of secondary significance, while the layer claimed that nothing outside may be true or bad. That compromise consisted in the uniquely Stoic belief that outside goods are of ethically impartial value, however are nevertheless the item of natural ambitions.

Zeno devised a three-part study of Stoic philosophy: physics, ethics, and logic. The ethics was essentially a moderate version of Cynicism; the physics was influenced by Plato's Timaeus and included a universe pervaded by an active, that is deliberate and a passive principle, as well as a cosmic web of reason and effect; and the logic comprised both formal logic and epistemology, which was empiricist-naturalistic for the Stoics.

Following Zeno, the Stoics disputed on a variety of problems, sometimes misinterpreting Zeno's ideas. The dispute between Cleanthes and Chrysippus about the unity of the virtues is perhaps the most excellent illustration: Zeno had talked about each virtue being some kind of knowledge, which Cleanthes construed in a strict unitary sense (that is, all virtues are the same, which implies wisdom, whereas Chrysippus interpreted in a more pluralistic sense, that is, every virtue is a branch of wisdom.

In defending Zeno's ideas, the early Stoics might be fiercely anti-empirical, as when Chrysippus persisted on supporting the concept that the heart, not the brain, is indeed the center of intellect. This ran counter to rather clear anatomical data that was already known in the Hellenistic period, earning the Stoics Galen's derision, but subsequent Stoics did alter their thinking on the subject. Despite this blunder, Chrysippus was arguably the most influential Stoic thinker, being responsible for a complete overhaul of the school, which had deteriorated under Cleanthes' leadership, a broad systematization of its teachings, and the introduction of a number of novel logic concepts—the facet of Stoicism that's had the most practical philosophical impact later on. "But for Chrysippus, there had been no Porch," said Diogenes Laertius.

STOICISM OF THE ROMANS

If the heads of various philosophical schools' journey to Rome in 155 B.C.E. was important in bringing philosophy to the Romans' notice, the political events of 88-86 B.C.E. altered the direction of Western philosophical thought, and Stoicism in specifically, for the rest of antiquity. Athens was ruled by philosophers at the period, especially the Peripatetic Athenion and, strangely, the Epicurean Aristion, who made the critical mistake of collaborating with Mithridates against Rome. The fall of the Monarch of Pontus, and hence of Athens, bode doom for the latter, resulting in a philosophical emigration across the Mediterranean.

The Middle Stoa thrived in the 2nd through early 1st century BCE, and was controlled by two Rhodes philosophers: Panaetius, its creator, and his follower Poseidonius. Before departing to Athens, Panaetius established a Stoic school in Rome, and Poseidonius was chiefly responsible for emphasizing the doctrine's religious aspects. Both were critical of Chrysippus' ethical ideas, believing that he had wandered too far from Stoicism's Platonic and Aristotelian foundations. It's possible that the Stoa in Rome devoted so much attention to moral and religious concerns within the Stoic worldview because Panaetius and Poseidonius spent so much time there. Cicero held Panaetius in high respect and utilized him as a reference for his own writing. Poseidonius, a student of Panaetius in Athens, instructed Cicero at his school on Rhodes before moving to Rome and staying with Cicero for a period. Poseidonius liked Plato and Aristotle, but he was particularly interested in natural and providential phenomena, unlike the majority of his school. Cicero most likely followed Poseidonius in articulating the Stoic theory in the second book of De natura deorum. Because his mentor, Panaetius, was primarily concerned with conceptions of duty and responsibility, Cicero's De officiis (was based on his studies.

If Chrysippus deserves credit for his perseverance in upholding Stoic logic and philosophy against the New Academy's Skepticism (3rd–2nd century BCE), it was Panaetius and Poseidonius who have been primarily responsible for Stoicism's great appeal in Rome. To the very practical Romans, it was exactly their turning of doctrine to problems in natural science and moral philosophy that appealed. Perhaps the times needed such pursuits, and with them, Stoicism evolved into primarily a philosophy for the individuals, demonstrating how to be stoic in the face of life's vagaries. Stoicism's main areas of concern at the period were law, global citizenship, creation, and the beneficent workings of providence and divine reason.

Stoicism grew popular in Rome during the difficult transition from the late Republic to the Empire, with Cato the Younger serving as a role model for younger Stoics due to his political resistance to Julius Caesar, the "tyrant." Athenodorus of Tarsus and Arius Didymus, two Stoic philosophers from the late First Century B.C.E., are cited by Sedley as forerunners of Seneca, one of the greatest and most contentious Stoic leaders. Both Athenodorus and Arius were personal counsellors to Augustus, the first emperor, and Arius even penned a letter of comfort to Augustus' wife, discussing the passing of her son, which Seneca later heralded as a reference work of emotional treatment, a field in which he himself engaged and became famous.

In the works of Lucius Seneca, a Roman statesman; Marcus Aurelius, a Roman emperor, and Epictetus, a former slave; such practical inclinations are vividly shown in the latter era of the school. Seneca's Epistulae morales (Moral Letters) and Libri morales (Moral Essays) emphasize the new orientation in Stoic ism in both style and content. Epictetus' Encheiridion (Manual) and Marcus Aurelius' Meditations advanced the Stoic message's majestic and yet personal comfort, while also demonstrating the strength of the Stoic message's rivalry with the new Christianity's developing authority. In these pieces, the sign of a guide, of a religious instructor, is prominent. The degree of Stoic influence during the first part of the second century CE, however, is impossible to determine with any certainty. These views had grown so popular that numerous Stoic terminology such as proper reason, understanding, acquiescence, indifference, natural law, and logos, as well as the concept of the wise person, were often utilized in debates and intellectual disagreements.

THE STOIC TRADITION

The stoic tradition refers to an expository illustration of the basic knowledge of Stoicism and all what it entails, its application and impacts on the lives of people. Stoicism is a philosophy that is constantly evolving. That is to say, Stoic philosophy is more than merely a collection of brilliant ideas arranged into a comprehensive and cohesive picture of reality. It is first a way of life, a practical implementation of ancient knowledge, and a guide to the decisions one makes in this life. It was the only ideology targeted to all human beings – regardless of gender, ethnicity, or socioeconomic status – from the outset. Women and slaves were invited to follow this road, to be regarded as brothers and sisters, a concept mocked by other philosophers who, like Aristotle, placed them somewhere between brutal creatures and free men.

Stoicism is still alive and well. It has survived for over 2300 years because it is globally flexible and accessible to individuals of all races, classes, and cultures. And there's more: it changes with time. Our ideology evolves in tandem with the human race's learning and growth. It develops as a result of the Stoics' own strength and commitment. Independent thought is a Stoic heritage, and we prefer it that way. As Seneca observed, members of the Stoic tradition do not obey a tyrant. This isn't to suggest that Stoics do have an eclectic collection of disparate ideas strewn about. It isn't the case. Its orthodoxy's fundamental core evolves slowly, glacially, growing and refining through time. It has a solid basis since it is based on the strength of a single idea: "the objective of life is to live in harmony with nature."

The Stoic's maxim is to live in harmony with nature, in accordance with nature, and according to nature. The Stoic school's founder, Zeno of Citium, invented the word and notion, but he wasn't alone. He was following in the footsteps of Heraclitus and Socrates, two of the greatest intellectuals in Western history. Zeno is the Stoic school's Father, while Heraclitus and Socrates are the Stoic school's Grandfathers.

In order to fully grasp every aspect of the Stoic's tradition, it is important that more explanations are made to every topic and issues of concern as regards to Stoicism. This also serves the purpose of providing answers to possible question that comes with trying to understand what Stoicism is.

- **Stoicism in more simple terms**

Stoicism is a school of thought that focuses on wisdom. That is, it is a philosophy on how to live a good life. About 2300 years ago, a man named Zeno created this philosophy in Athens, Greece. After several years of study with the Cynics, he attended Plato's Academy before establishing his own school near the Athens central market. Zeno began his school of philosophy by standing on a market porch and conversing with passers-by. He eventually gathered a regular group of persons to stand at his side and discuss philosophy. His school was the porch. The Greek term for porch is *Stoa*, and the men who gathered there to discuss philosophy were known as the porch men, or Stoics. Stoicism existed for approximately 500 years as the leading philosophy of ancient Greece and Rome. It resurfaced as a popular ideology during the Renaissance, when individuals sought solutions to life's questions via reason rather than religion. The Stoics concept, as well as those who follow it, are still alive and thriving today all across the world.

- **Effects of stoicism on emotions and feelings**

One of the common questions on Stoicism is on whether it represses emotions and feelings. The appropriate answer to this is No, it is merely an old misconception. Emotions and sentiments are natural and acceptable, and they're sometimes even necessary for our existence. There are instances when succumbing to fear and fleeing is the best option.

The Stoic concept that emotions are founded on a judgment is the source of the mistake. We all have emotional reactions to situations that might produce wrath, sadness, and fear, including Stoics, but it is our evaluation about the incident that either stirs up or cools the feeling after the initial intuitive reaction. "There really is nothing either positively or negatively, but mentality makes it so," Shakespeare remarked in Hamlet. Shakespeare, by the way, was a student of Stoic philosophy and frequently employed Stoic themes in his plays.

We think that it is our judgment, not the object itself, that determines whether something is good or evil. If we are dissatisfied, it was a judgment that triggered our feelings and caused us to be sad. Everyone wants to be happy, and Stoicism is all concerned with maximizing happiness and living well.

- **The meaning of the stoic's maxim: "live according to nature."**

Zeno, who was the pioneer of Stoicism, was also the first to introduce the phrase "live according to Nature," which simply implies that Stoics utilize Nature as a guide in their lives. Nature, we think, teaches us all we need to understand about living properly in this world. It is for this reason why Stoic physics is so crucial. Natural philosophy was the name given to physics in ancient, and through studying nature, we may learn about ourselves and what makes us feel good, prosperous, and smart.

Later, Panaetius, another renowned Stoic, broadened the initial motto to encompass not only nature generally, but also the individual's nature. Everybody has a distinct personality, with various traits and capacities that we may cultivate in order to realize our ultimate ideal. As a result, living in accordance with Nature also entails living in harmony with one's own nature. "If you have adopted any character beyond your power, you have both degraded yourself in that, and disregarded one that you might have fulfilled with success," Epictetus, a Roman Stoic instructor, observed. The prudent live in accordance with both the nature of human in general and one's own unique character.

- **Stoicism's perception of good and bad**

Good is always the only virtue, and only virtuelessness is always bad. Stoics do not think that there is any evil in nature; rather, we believe that there is evil in human conduct, which occurs when individuals choose to do things that are destructive to themselves. Stoics don't believe anyone can hurt you; instead, it is believed that you may injure yourself by refusing to live in accordance with nature. However, we do not judge others for their lack of virtue since they are already penalizing themselves by their actions.
No one can harm you since you are alone accountable for your character's nobility, and that noble character is the Stoic's ultimate goal. Wealthy women and men abound, but noble character is the rarest and most valuable of all. Stoicism instructs you on how to develop a noble personality.

- **Stoics' beliefs in God**

All Stoics believe in God in some ways, yes, but they do so in different ways. Because nature is their deity, all Stoics are pantheists, they may be deists, atheists, or agnostics and yet be Stoics in top form. The type of Stoic you are is determined by whether you believe nature's wisdom and processes are conscious or unconscious. Is nature aware of itself or not? Human beings are conscious beings who were formed by nature. Are we the only conscious ones, or is our maker equally conscious?
Nature, according to the early Stoics, was both predetermined and conscious. Those were the beliefs of the deists, although there were a few who claimed that nature was unconscious when Stoicism was accepted in ancient Rome. Those with such belief were the earliest atheists among the Stoics. Today, there are agnostics, deists, and atheists among the Stoics. This kind of variety is absolutely okay. There is a huge tent in the Stoic community, and debating is tolerated inside it.

- **Stoics enjoyment of such delights as fine cuisine, art, wine, music, and making love etc.**

Without a doubt, Stoics consider themselves to be pantheists. Their God is everywhere. They treasure their reasons above everything else since it is a unique gift by Nature, however their creator may also be found in our eyes, ears, nose, taste buds, and kinaesthetic sense, and also in their minds.

- **Beliefs on life after death**

Stoics do not belief there is a single correct solution to this belief. There are two approaches to use if one is seeking for clarity. The most reliable method is for the person to die, at which point he or she will be certain. The alternative, and somewhat less dramatic, option is to embrace a religious organisation that offers eternal life. Unfortunately, they are unable to back up their claim. If you believe in a religion, such as Christianity or Islam, you will be told what you should understand regarding life after death. Nothing is certain if you seek reason, proof, or evidence. Stoicism cannot empirically confirm or refute life after death in any manner. No one is capable. Religions that teach differently encourage you to believe in myths, stories, and optimism. Such confidence is never required by the Stoics' worldview. There have always been differences over this because Stoics are often more satisfied with conflict than with faith. They are basically agnostic about life after death, but can all agree on one thing, though: if one lives according to Nature in this life, he or she is unlikely to have anything to fret over in the next life, if there is.

- **Why the world needs a stoic community**

First and foremost, humans are social animals. That is how we are wired. Humans are happier and more successful when we have friends and families to look after and who look after us and provide us with a sense of purpose in life. It's always been like this, and it'll probably always be like this. The majority of us now live in cities, which has resulted in a sense of isolation and alienation. For majority, or even all of us, our ancient yearning to relate has been undermined, and it is a significant loss. We've been part of a tribe or a group for at least as long as we've been as a separate species, if not millions of years. It's ingrained in our DNA and bones. The Stoic communities restore us to our true nature as social animals, allowing us to live in the world as it is while yet having a group to support and share our ideals.

- **Stoicism's perspective on racial and gender issues**

Because of our philosophy's heritage and teachings, this is one of the crucial matters. Only the Stoics were fully educated when it came to race and gender matters. Other ideas were frequently mocked and disparaged, but Stoicism have always maintained that all humans are equal. Also, homosexuality was never a problem in ancient Greece when Stoicism was created, and it still isn't now.

Stoics were actually the first to denounce rape, which is a fact not well known. "The God of Eros, love, made me do it," was mostly the explanation for rape during a time when it was considerably more widespread than it is today's world. That justification, according to the Stoics, was folly. Rape was a bad idea. You DO have the ability to fight back. None of us have the right to abuse another person's body, and no deity can force you to act poorly. There are no justifications. Of course, we still hold that belief today.

Returning to the subject of equality, reason is the key. Posidonius, antiquity's greatest scientist, travelled broadly and explored many distinctive people and cultures, confirming what Stoics have always believed that humans are the same everywhere, and our greatest faculty, our capacity to reason, is what unites all of us, no matter how different we may look.

THE STOIC PHILOSOPHERS

Agasicles, the Spartan king, famously joked that he wished to be the pupil of men whose son he would also like to be. It's therefore an important factor to consider while looking for role models. Stoicism is no different. Before we commence our research, we must ask ourselves, about the people who followed these rules, those that can be used as examples, and those who we can look up to.

Several great philosophers in history have greatly contributed to the success of Stoicism as the great philosophy it is, especially to its widespread use in the world at large. These philosophers include Zeno of Citium - the founder, Cleanthes - the studious successor of Zeno, Chrysippus – Stoicism's second founder, Diogenes of Babylon – who connected the Stoicism of Greece and Rome, Panaetus of Rhodes – Who was a radical Stoic, Seneca the Younger – the most controversial thinker of Stoicism, Epictectus – A model Stoic philosopher, and Marcus Aurelius – Stoicism's emperor. These philosophers and their various contributions to Stoicism will be further explained.

Seneca, Musonius Rufus, Epictetus, and Marcus Aurelius are the four Roman Stoics whose writings and teachings have lasted nearly two millennia and are now the core of Stoicism. Over a thousand works on Stoic philosophy are supposed to have been published, but only a few have survived—mostly those authored by these geniuses. Fortunately, these bright but imperfect individuals did not dwell in caves deep in the mountains; instead, they were actively involved in society and actively worked to improve the world. You'll meet an extremely wealthy dramatist, the forerunner of today's entrepreneur, an early feminist, and a disabled slave who should be the Roman Emperor's major influence and the world's mightiest person.

- **Zeno of Citium – Founder of Stoicism**

Some facts have been established and explained in the previous introductory parts of this book about Zeno of Citium, who founded Stoicism. However, there are several other facts that should be further explained in under to fully capture his works and how he founded Stoicism.

In roughly 300 BCE, Zeno of Citium founded his own school of philosophy in Athens, which became known as Stoicism. Zeno was a rich Phoenician trader before establishing his school. Zeno, on the other hand, travelled to Athens after escaping from a shipwreck on a commercial expedition in search of the greatest way to live. Zeno inquired the shopkeeper where he could locate someone comparable while standing in a bookshop examining some intellectual volumes on Socrates. Crates the Cynic, the shopkeeper said, pointing to a weird hermit-like guy passing by. Crates, as a Cynic, shunned worldly comfort and instead led an austere existence, unconcerned about his untidy appearance. Zeno could not get over his apprehensions about the Cynic way of life despite learning under Crates, so Crates designed a lecture for him. He gave Zeno the task of lugging a pot of lentil stew throughout town. Zeno tried to hide the pot because he was embarrassed, so Crates whacked his cane and smashed the urn. Zeno fled in humiliation, covered in stew, as Crates yelled, "Why flee, my little Phoenician?" Nothing bad has happened to you." Zeno intended to build a philosophy that merged Cynic principles with a more humble and civilized manner of life, bringing satisfaction to those who followed it. Zeno started teaching his own beliefs from beneath the Stoa Poikile, a coloured colonnade in Athens, after learning under several philosophers. Eventually, his students grew in number, and the Stoic school was founded.

Zeno created many of Stoicism's key principles in those initial periods, such as the view that God and the cosmos were the same thing. He also established Stoicism as a philosophy dedicated to discovering "the good life," one lived in harmony with virtue and nature. Zeno's students, on the other hand, were responsible for turning Stoicism into one of the most lasting philosophies of the ancient world.

- **Cleanthes - Zeno's Inquisitive Successor**

Cleanthes replaced Zeno as the head of the Stoic school when he died in 262 BCE. Cleanthes, a former boxer who enjoyed working with his hands, had gone to Athens to study philosophy. Cleanthes became interested in Stoicism after hearing lectures from both Zeno and Crates. Cleanthes went on to further expand Stoicism by combining his theories on ethics, metaphysics, and logic into one philosophy. He accepted the reality of the soul and incorporated it into Stoic views about how life should be lived. Cleanthes proposed that the sun was created from the pneuma, or divine fire, that composed the cosmos, based on Zeno's concept of the divine logos. He thought that the sun must be an emanation of the divine logos since it provided life to creatures on Earth.

Cleanthes had a different approach to ethics than Zeno. He felt that pleasure was at odds with nature, and that feelings were frailties that lacked the might of the divine logos-created souls. Rather than pursuing enjoyment, Cleanthes called for a life of constancy. Reason and rationality were the only constants for Cleanthes. Embracing the divine logos' universal reason and surrendering to fate required accepting the divine logos' universal reason.

- **Chryssipus – Stoicism's Second Founder**

Under Chrysippus, who thought that fate dictated everything in the cosmos, the Stoic concept of fate advanced significantly. Chrysippus utilized his own groundbreaking system of logical premises to demonstrate that nothing can occur without a definite reason because things and situations can only be true or untrue. Rival philosophers claimed that a deterministic cosmos contradicts the concept of free choice, but Chrysippus disagreed, claiming that simple and complicated destiny existed. Human activities have the potential to alter the outcome of ostensibly inescapable occurrences. We may suffer from disease as a result of predetermined fate, but our responses to the situation are entirely our own. These reactions are part of our inborn nature, which the divine Logos has bestowed upon us. Stoic ethics drifted away from Cleanthes' impersonal, logical ends and toward something more personal under Chrysippus. Living in line with our natural rational perceptions of nature became the purpose of life for Chrysippus.

Chrysippus, like Cleanthes, advocated perfect emotional control in order to achieve a condition of inner serenity known as ataraxia. Chrysippus thought that we may use logic and reason in preparation for circumstances in which we are confronted with strong emotions so that we are not overwhelmed. Chrysippus died in 206 BCE, with Stoicism well on its way to becoming the major philosophy of the later Roman Empire. According to legend, Chrysippus died of laughter after drinking wine excessively that hadn't been diluted.

- **Diogenes – who connected the Greece and Rome Stoicisms**

The Roman Republic started battling the Greek countries for control in the Mediterranean from 200 BCE, eventually conquering the region in 146 BCE. During this period, Greek concepts impacted the Romans, who expanded on the Hellenistic World's foundations. Philosophy was one of the Greek ideals that the Romans adopted, and three rivals tried to acquire momentum in Rome. The Greeks sent three contending philosophers to Rome around 155 BCE to protest a high punishment levied by the Romans. Critolaus the Peripatetic, Carneades the Skeptic, and Diogenes of Babylon, who stood for the Stoics, were among these thinkers. Each philosopher delivered a speech in the hopes of persuading the Roman Council to reverse the fine. Carneades delivered two speeches, one praising and the other criticizing the Roman judiciary system. This enraged the Romans, so he was sacked as a result. Critolaus contended that enjoyment was a vice, which the assembly did not agree with. The Romans were interested in Stoicism after hearing Diogenes' lecture, which was appreciated for its calm and humble manner. Diogenes left for Athens when the fine was waived. He remained the leader of the Stoic school until roughly 140 BCE, when he died. Diogenes' biggest contribution, despite being a prolific writer, was spreading the Stoic ideals to Rome.

- **Panaetius of Rhodes – A Radical Stoic**

Diogenes the Babylonian may have brought Stoicism to the Romans Panaetius of Rhodes was the one who genuinely disseminated it. Panaetius was born in Rhodes in 185 BCE and came to Athens as a young man to study with Diogenes and other philosophers of Stoicism. After learning as much as he could from the Stoics, Panaetius met Scipio Aemilianus, a visiting Roman statesman. When Scipio left for Rome, Panaetius followed in his footsteps and began authoring a number of important Stoic works. These works spread across Rome, influencing important leaders like Cicero. Within Stoicism, Panaetius was a radical, rejecting many established concepts and inventing his own views. He simplified Stoic philosophy, giving it a new lease on life. Prior to Panaetius, most Stoics thought that pneuma, or divine fire, was the universe's fundamental element. They said that the cosmos will undergo a systematic process of annihilation and rebirth known as the conflagration, in which everything would be annihilated and the universe would begin all over again. Panaetius objected to is pessimistic viewpoint and ceased to teach it.

Another classic Stoic principle that Panaetius contended with was apatheia, or the technique of suppressing emotions. Some feelings and pleasures, he claimed, did not conflict with living in line with man's logical nature. Given his effect on the following generation of Roman Stoics, Panaetius is unquestionably one of the school's most influential philosophers. Panaetius lived around 110 BCE and was one of the last teachers of the Stoic school.

- **Seneca the Younger – Dramatist and Roman Statesman**

Lucius Annaeus Seneca, also known as Seneca the Younger or just Seneca, was a controversial Stoic philosopher who was born in Cordoba, Spain, around the time of Jesus and educated at Rome, Italy. He is regarded as one of antiquity's greatest authors, and many of his articles and personal correspondence have survived and are valuable sources of Stoic philosophy. These writings communicate to us since he concentrated on the practical aspects of Stoicism, such as how to travel, how to deal with hardships and its triggered emotions such as anger or grief, how to manage oneself while committing suicide, which he was ordered to do, how to cope with wealth, which he only knew so well, and how to deal with poverty.

Seneca the Younger was a Roman statesman and playwright who lived from 4BC to 65AD. He was Emperor Nero's mentor and subsequently counsellor. This last point may lead the uninitiated reader to believe that Stoic Philosophy was involved in the horrible reign of the legendary tyrant Nero, but the truth is that Seneca was executed for his role in a plot to murder Nero. As a result, it appears that the Stoic Philosophical beliefs did not agree with Emperor Nero's heinous acts.

Although Seneca worked for a small group of educated people and typically dedicated his works to a specific friend or family, his letters and essays demonstrate a Stoicism that may be applied to a larger audience. He was an instructor who agreed with the most significant features of Stoicism while also disagreeing with some of its other components. Seneca was not a philosopher in the pattern of Epictetus, who we shall study later, as he was a powerful and rich man who was prone to occasional displays of arrogance and conceit. He was quite adept of humility, and once defined himself as "a long way from becoming an acceptable, much alone a flawless human person," despite making immodest comments about his own growth in his works.

It's tough to pass a final verdict on Seneca the younger's life. The impact of his Stoic writings on a variety of academic fields is undeniable. If he is to be chastised in any manner, it will be for his connection with a government that operated in opposition to Stoic Philosophy's ideals. Whether Seneca was a hypocrite or not, He lived a tumultuous life filled with wealth and power, as well as philosophy and reflection, he knew well enough that he was not perfect. Stoicism was constant throughout his life, as seen by the many helpful and encouraging letters he wrote.

- **Musonius Rufus**

Gaius Musonius Rufus, the least well-known of the Roman Stoics, founded his own school where he taught Stoic philosophy. Because he didn't care to write anything down, very little is known about his life and teachings. Fortunately, throughout the lectures, one of Musonius' students, Lucius, took notes. Rufus pushed for a philosophy that was both practical and lived. "Just as medical research is useless unless it leads to the health of human body," he said, "philosophical theory is useless unless it contributes to the virtue of the human spirit." He gave specific instructions on dietary habits, sex life, suitable attire, and how to treat one's parents. He believed philosophy should not only be very practical, but also global. He claimed that education and philosophical research may help both men and women.

At the time, Musonius Rufus was the most important Stoic instructor, and his impact in Rome was well-known. Emperor Nero deported him to the Greek island of Gyaros in 65 CE because he was too despotic. Gyaros, which was a desert-like island, would have suited considerably better with Seneca's description of Corsica as a "barren and thorny rock." Musonius returned to Rome after Nero's death in 68 CE before being exiled again. He died about the year 100 CE, leaving behind not just a few lecture notes from Lucius, but also his most renowned pupil, Epictetus, who, as we'll see later, went on to become a powerful Stoic instructor.

- **Epictetus – A Model Stoic Philosopher**

Epictetus is a fascinating historical character and Stoic thinker whose life lessons are still relevant in the twenty-first century, despite the culture differences from his time. Epictetus was born in Hierapolis as a slave, which in present day is in Pamukkale in Turkey. If he had a genuine name, it is unknown. Epictetus is a Greek word that meaning "property" or "purchased item." Epaphroditos, a rich freedman, that is, a former slave who served as a secretary to Emperor Nero in Rome, where Epictetus spent his boyhood, purchased him. He was born with one leg amputated or suffered an injury from a past master. Epaphroditos, his newfound master, was kind to him and enabled him to study Stoicism under Musonius Rufus the best teacher in Rome.

Epictetus was released by his lord sometime after Nero's death in 68 CE, which was a normal occurrence in Rome with intellectual and learned slaves. Epictetus started teaching philosophy after gaining his freedom. Emperor Domitian prohibited philosophy in 93 CE, so Epictetus left Rome to start a philosophical college in Nicopolis, Greece. Epictetus lived a humble life, avoiding worldly possessions and dedicating himself to promoting Stoicism. Stoicism recovered credibility and popularity among the Romans after Domitian's murder. Epictetus, the foremost Stoic instructor at the time, had the option of returning to Rome, but he decided to remain at Nicopolis, until his death in about 135 CE. Epictetus, like his instructor Musonius Rufus, did not write down anything. Fortunately, there was another nerd among the pupils, Arrian, who took meticulous notes and composed the renowned Discourses, which were a collection of excerpts from Epictetus' lectures. Arrian also composed the Enchiridion, a brief summary of the Discourses' most essential concepts. Enchiridion is sometimes mistranslated as Handbook, although it properly means "always at hand", which is constantly ready to face life's problems.

- **Marcus Aurelius – An Emperor of Stoicism**

Marcus Aurelius, the Roman emperor from 121 to 180 AD, is the most well-known Stoic of all time. He was the last of the "Five Good Emperors," and his life has been chronicled in a number of historical works and even modern films. As a philosopher, he is best known for the Meditations of Marcus Aurelius, which is the most historically important source on the writings and doctrines of the early Stoic Philosophers available today. Marcus is reported to have liked hobbies such as boxing, wrestling, and hunting as a youth, as well as philosophy. He studied with several philosophers, one of them loaned him a copy of Epictetus' Discourses, which became his single most influential work. Emperor Hadrian adopted Marcus' maternal uncle Antoninus when he was sixteen, and Antoninus in turn adopted Marcus. Marcus' political authority did not get to his head when he entered palace life, either as a co-emperor of his adoptive father or as an emperor after Antoninus' death. He used his authority and money with tremendous moderation. He also opted not to use his influence to preach Stoicism and educate his fellow Romans on the merits of its practices, despite his enthusiasm in the philosophy. He was a very good emperor who reigned from 161 to 180 CE and was the last of a line of monarchs referred to as the Five Good Emperors.

The Meditations of Marcus Aurelius are organized into twelve volumes, each embodying lessons from different times of his life. Although it is thought that Marcus Aurelius composed these works only for his personal benefit, they have become a must-read for all Stoic philosophers. The Meditations' writing style is basic and communicative, making it easy to understand for novice students. For centuries, The Meditations is regarded as one of Stoicism's key writings, and it continues to influence politicians and philosophers today.

1
UNDERSTANDING THE PRINCIPLES AND CONCEPTS OF STOICISM

THE OBJECTIVES OF STOICISM

"Follow and obey nature," has been the most popular saying related to the Stoic's philosophy. Is following nature, then, Stoicism's main objective? Is it to live a happy life and acquire peace of mind? Is it to help you grow in character? Is it even feasible that all of these things are connected? So, what is the main objective? Happiness, also known as eudaimonia, is the ultimate objective. As a result, to live a happy life, that is what we're all chasing, whether we recognize it or not, the Stoics and many other antique thinkers will remark. That's exactly what the whole thing about Stoicism is aiming towards. Another question is how does a person go about doing that? Well, you do it by honing your personality. You do it by cultivating such characteristics and excellences. What steps do you take to become a good person? By cultivating the wonderful character attributes that distinguish a good person. But it also entails honing your reasoning, which they believe is one of the most important aspects of a person. It entails avoiding unpleasant emotions and so avoiding the "mental ailments" of illogical emotions. Then, living in peace with nature is linked to this in two ways. In one method, as we discussed before, person can live a perfect flow of life by syncing your will with nature's will. If you're continuously at odds with nature, how can you have a decent, happy, quiet, satisfied life? To avoid disharmony, you must live in harmony with nature. However, there is a way in which living in accordance with environment is inextricably linked to the endeavour of attempting to comprehend nature. Trying to understand how nature operates. The Stoics would be dedicated to the generally Aristotelian concept that humans are inherently sensible, inquiring beings after they had that information – once they had done that work. You must use your reason if you are to be a good person, and part of that will be attempting to comprehend the world surrounding you. That's just what a nice, sensible person would do.

Stoicism's ultimate purpose is to grow the mind to the point that the practitioner achieves eudaimonia, a condition of being. Eudaimonia is a Greek concept that loosely translates as thriving, success, or happiness; a condition in which the Stoic is free from the shackles of unnecessary suffering to the greatest extent possible. Stoics who live in this condition rely only on their internal state of mind for happiness, rather than the uncontrolled environment. A person who has acquired eudaimonia was referred to be a sage by the Stoics. The Stoic sage was someone who has made himself resistant to hardship produced by external circumstances via virtue and reason. Their happiness is solely dependent on what they can control, such as their behaviours, values, beliefs, and perspectives. Wealth, prestige, respect, and continual comfort are not among them.

The Stoic sage's beliefs are an ideal; it's doubtful that philosophers can reach this degree of self-mastery for more than just few hours at a stretch, but it serves as a useful benchmark for us to strive for in our practice. According to Stoicism, the objective of achieving eudaimonia is reached through behaving with virtue in the world and understanding it with reason and logic.

THE MAIN PRINCIPLES OF STOICISM

Over antiquity, the Stoic philosophy evolved, turning from physics and logic to more psychological matters like serenity and well-being. Furthermore, while the Stoics never could agree on all of its tenets, there are fundamental concepts at the heart of the Stoic system of operation. Some of the Stoics' most essential principles and practices for living a happier life will be further explained. Importantly, they aren't just intriguing concepts to mull about and then dismiss; they're supposed to be put into practice every day of a person's life.

The Stoic philosophers had major ethical beliefs, some of which ae explained below.

- **Nature:** Nature, on the other hand, is logical.
- **Virtue:** A life lived in accordance with reason is virtuous.
- **Law of Reason:** The law of reason governs everything in the world. Humans cannot genuinely escape its inevitable force, but they may, for the first time, consciously follow the rule.
- **Apathea:** Because desire is illogical, life should be fought like a war. Excessive emotion should be avoided.
- **Wisdom:** It is the foundational virtue. The cardinal qualities of wisdom, courage, justice, and self-control, come from it.
- **Pleasure:** It is neither a good nor a negative thing. It's only allowed if it doesn't get in the way of pursuing virtue.
- **Duty:** Virtue should indeed be pursued for the purpose of duty, not pleasure.
- **Evil:** Poverty, disease, and death are really not inherently wicked.

With the above explanations, we arrive at the expositions of some core Stoic principles and practices.

1. Concentrate on what you have control over

Differentiating between what we can alter and what we can't change is the single most essential discipline in Stoic philosophy. What we have a say in and what we don't. We all waste much too much time and energy fretting about things we can't change. When it comes to time, how much is enough? The Stoics would respond, "Anything greater than zero." This is because attempting to influence things you don't have control over is a pointless endeavour that comes at the price of taking action on the things you do have control over.

Furthermore, even worrying about such matters produces undue stress. Here, Stoicism agrees with Buddhism, which holds that suffering is equal to pain multiplied by resistance. The only rational option is to accept the things you can't alter.

For instance, when a delay is caused due to bad weather, ranting at an airline employee won't help. There's no way to make yourself shorter or taller or to be born in a foreign nation by wishing. You can't make someone love you, irrespective of your effort. So learn to tell the difference between what you can actually control and what you can't. Wherever you are able to respond, that is where you should concentrate your efforts. In a nutshell, this means focusing on yourself, your own ideas and habits, rather than critiquing others. We would all be happier, both emotionally and financially, if we focused our efforts improving the areas we have control over.

2. Be a person of great virtues

"A good character is the sole guarantee of permanent, blissful enjoyment," Seneca famously stated. Virtue is significantly more essential to Stoics than pleasure. A good life is one that is characterized by virtue. In other words, the way to real happiness is a principled life of dignity, ethical conduct, and service, not a selfish pursuit of pleasure. Stoics believe that virtue is both adequate and required for pleasure in all circumstances. The Stoics place a high importance on eudaimonia, or well-being—the excellent life rather than a pleasant mood. The Stoics, on the other hand, think that virtue leads to happiness and peace of mind. As a byproduct of virtue, several positive outcomes occur. To put it another way, the Stoics' fundamental duty is to be useful to others and serve the common good, not to make themselves happy. They do this because it's the natural and correct thing to do. But, as it turns out, doing things in that attitude makes people happy. So, living a life of virtue is beneficial. These virtues include: Wisdom, courage, justice, and temperance, which are the four most important virtues.

Courage, or bravery, refers to more than only the kind of bravery shown in war or as a fireman. It entails a willingness to confront tough and painful situations head-on. An awkward discussion, the loss of a career, or the loss of a loved one are all possibilities.

Temperance, or moderation, does not only imply abstaining from drugs and alcohol, but in the perspective of a Stoic, intoxication is clearly not good. Temperance here refers to avoiding all forms of excess, including luxury, food, and leisure. One can exercise excessively, think excessively, read excessively, work excessively, or be bold to the point of folly. All of these excesses need restraint.

Doing what is just, even if it is uncomfortable, tough, or costly, is what justice entails. When the circumstance calls for it, try to do the right thing. Treat others the same way you want to be treated. And remember that every minor decision and detail is a chance to put these broader concepts into effect.

"Wisdom" denotes "truth and comprehension" in this context. A Stoic should strive to discover the truth, continue to study, and retain an open mind. However, the objective is to seek the most significant truth, those that are most relevant to leading a happy life, because this will lead to understanding of the actual nature of things.

Marcus Aurelius once stated, "Your mind will be like its frequent ideas; for the soul gets stained with the colour of its thoughts." Living a life of virtue, on the other hand, does not imply being judgemental and self-righteous.

3. Make a move.

When you think of a "stoic" individual in the traditional sense, you could think of someone who sits nonchalantly, statuesque, and unmoved to activity. This isn't a Stoic philosophy. The Stoics placed a strong emphasis on making moves. This is a direct consequence of the first principle. After determining what you can and cannot affect, you focus all of your efforts on the things you can. You're not going to be a helpless victim of your situations. You put forth a lot of effort to improve your life and the world around you. You are a proactive person. You keep going even when you are going through Hell. However, action should not be done arbitrarily. It must be purposeful activity, guided by well selected aims and principles. To put it another way, a Stoic aspires to be virtuously active.

4. Set a Good Example
"On no account call yourself a philosopher, and do not speak much among the uninstructed about theorems, but practice what follows from them," Epictetus said. At a feast, for example, don't tell how a guy should eat, instead eat as you should." People will learn a lot more by seeing you live than they will from any teaching you may offer them. This is due not just to the fact that humans and many other animals learn by imitating others, but also to the fact that people become defensive when they are told what to do. If someone teaches me how to be a better person, for example, the inference is that I am not currently a decent person. I get stubborn when I feel judged. However, if someone demonstrates how to be a better person just by living their own life, I may be encouraged to follow their lead. My negative reaction to being told how to improve myself is a manifestation of my inflated ego.

5. You have no right to anything.
Genuine Stoics have goals they want to reach and work hard to accomplish them, but they also recognize that they are not entitled to prosperity. This is related to Stoicism's first principle. You have the option of selecting a target. You have complete control over how much energy you put in. You have complete control over the techniques you employ. However, because you can't control all of the factors, you can't control the result.
You can prepare for an athletic challenge to the best of your ability and give it your all, yet still come up short. It's possible to spend years creating a book in the hopes of it being a success, but there's no assurance that anybody will read it.
Goals are essential, as is hard effort, but no one is obligated to success. Please remember: working carefully for a goal you may never achieve is difficult.

6. Reduce your ego.
The Stoics are not talking about the "ego" in the Freudian sense. Rather, "an unbalanced confidence in your own significance" is what ego meant here. It's every person's petulant child, the one that prioritizes having his or her way over all else. The desire to outperform. It's a sense of assurance and dominance that goes beyond confidence and ability. Ego is a skewed perspective of your own abilities and significance, not reality-based confidence. It breeds arrogance, obstinacy, and irresponsibility.

Ego is the adversary of what you desire and what you have in this way: developing your skill. Of genuine inventiveness. Of being able to cooperate successfully with others. Of lengthy life. Advantages and opportunities are resisted. It attracts opponents and mistakes like a magnet.

The "do the opposite" approach is the most effective way to minimize ego. Feeling sluggish? Put up some effort. Are you under the impression that your lover owes you something? Be kind and generous to them. Consider what your ego desires and then do the polar opposite. Don't give it anything to feed on; starve it.

Don't worry about what other people are doing since your ego is concerned about being superior than them; instead, concentrate on your own task. Don't publish about your life on the internet just to brag about it, and don't scan through newsfeeds to match your life to other people's. Simply live your life according to your principles and aspirations. To put it another way, develop autonomous self-esteem.

The ego craves rapid gratification. Conquer this by gradually and continuously performing the task that means most to you, regardless of whether or not you receive any acknowledgment. This sends a message to your ego that its demands aren't significant. It loses power every time it hears the message. As a result, patiently working in anonymity is one practical cure to excessive ego. If you achieve popularity or earn awards later, that's great, but you'll still do the work.

7. When faced with failure, adversity, or tragedy, practice resilience.

Stoics avoid misfortune in the same manner that any sensible person would. But it does happen from time to time, and the Stoic purpose is to recognize hardship correctly and not let it undermine one's peace of mind. Indeed, the Stoic's goal is to accept setback without surprise and use it as fodder for the production of bigger things. Nobody loves difficulty in any situation, but it is a vital component in the development of honorable individuals and worthwhile achievements, which we do desire in the long run. Stoics look for value in everything that happens.

Believing that challenges are really opportunities is an auto prophecy: you will act in such a manner to show yourself correct if you believe this. You will fight to make your vision come true if you feel that suffering makes you stronger. Affirm to yourself, "It's all strong mental training," when anything unpleasant happens. Every moment, Epictetus emphasized, is a chance to exercise virtue. Every challenge and temptation is an opportunity to strengthen your resolve.

Stoics are naturally affected by difficulty, sorrow, and tragedy since they are human. They do, however, play the equanimity game, which involves returning to a calm state of mind as rapidly as possible. The more you commit yourself to play this game, the stronger you get at it, according to Marcus Aurelius:

"When life throws you a curve ball, don't waste time regaining your composure; don't stay out of tune for longer than you have to." Returning to the harmony on a regular basis will help you perfect it."

8. Be thankful.

"He who does not lament the things he does not have, but rejoices in the things he does have, is wise." Epictetus said. Despite the fact that the Stoics are unlikely to have kept gratitude notebooks, they believed in the significance of observing and acknowledging the many pleasant parts of life that we accept as normal.

'Practicing misfortune,' as the Stoics called it, is a surprising strategy for growing thankfulness. Deliberately experiencing some type of deprivation is one aspect of this. Allow yourself to go a day without eating. For a week, pretend you don't own a water heater and take cold showers. Take a trip to the woods and sleep on the ground. This type of uncomfortable training not only makes you stronger, but it also makes you less prone to take common conveniences for granted. It also aids in the development of your virtue by building empathy for the vast numbers of people who are forced to live in this manner on a daily basis.

Imagined disaster is another variation of this method. You can't go out and lose everything you care about in real life, but you may do the thought experiment. Consider how you'd grieve if you lost your job, house, or relationship. It will, at the very least, make you more appreciative for what you have. Imagining your own death is the most severe manifestation of this. The Stoic phrase 'memento mori,' which means 'remember death,' is popular among Stoics. One aim of the strategy is to become more at ease with your impending death, so you don't have to live in fear of it. Another goal is to make you feel more fortunate to be living and, as a response, live a better life. Because you might die at any moment, be humble and live a virtue-filled life.

9. Make use of your willpower.

Stoics aren't heartless; they just don't let emotions dictate their conduct. Irrespective of how they feel, they endeavour to do what is right. This is done for two reasons: First, It benefits everyone else, and Secondly, it benefits them.

"The greatest share of peace of mind is doing nothing wrong, those who lack self-control have confusing and unsettled lives." Seneca once said. You may learn to enjoy doing the right thing. Fast food, sugar, and narcotics may be substituted with salads, nature, and exercise, to satisfy your desires. Your ambition to obtain what you desire might be replaced with a desire to assist others in achieving their goals.

It's hard to believe, but your brain has the ability to rewire itself. If you modify your behaviour, your brain will ultimately change as well. Healthy and virtuous activities that previously sapped your willpower become effortless and routine in the long term. So when does willpower come into play the most? When everything is at its worst. When doing the right thing is the most difficult thing to do. When it seems difficult to keep your spirits up. That's when you'll need a lot of strong willpower.

10. Select a Response.

The discipline of responding rather than reacting is at the heart of Stoicism. How would you behave if you were confronted with a problem? You make the decision to respond with tenacity. When a bad idea pops into your head, do you react with criticism and judgement? You make the decision to reject that notion and replace it with a more positive one. Do you experience a sense of powerlessness that makes you feel hopeless? Regardless, you choose to take constructive action.

We don't have a chance to choose to act in line with reason and morality if all we do is react. To exercise our free will, we must create a gap between response and stimulus and intervene there. So, when you're upset by an occurrence in your life, take a step back and consider the larger picture. The universe is enormous. The issues that irritate us appear to be massive and vital. You can tell that they aren't if you zoom out.

THE IMPORTANT CONCEPTS OF STOIC PHILOSOPHY

The great works of the Roman Stoics focused on four major ideas that give accurate description of Stoicism. This section elaborates on how Zeno and other early Stoic philosophers explained the important concepts if the Stoic philosophy.

- **Virtue**

Zeno and the ancient Stoics believed that virtue is the only thing that lasts and matters in life. The ancient Stoics had a fairly detailed definition of virtue, which included justice, moderation, courage, and a general perfection of character as some of the most significant qualities. When considering the notion of Stoic virtue, it's important to note that the Stoics weren't only concerned in defining it as an academic concept; they were also interested in putting it into practice in real-life circumstances and relationships.

The only thing that is genuinely nice is a good mental state that is associated with morality and logic. This is the only way we can be sure of our pleasure. Money, prosperity, popularity, and other external factors can never offer us happiness. Though there's nothing improper with these things, and they have worth and may well be a part of a happy existence, the pursuit of them frequently harms the one thing that can offer us happiness: a decent, reasonable mental state.

The ancient Stoics also thought that everyone is born with the ability to identify virtue and differentiate right from wrong. This basic principle also produces the necessity to accept any responsibility for one's acts, and it became the cornerstone of other schools of thought, such as Roman intellectuals, who constructed Natural law teachings from these principles.

Wisdom, Courage, Temperance, and Justice were the four virtues that the Stoics believed in. We will take a look at each one:

THE FOUR STOIC VIRTUES

Courage, temperance, justice, and wisdom are the four Stoic virtues. In Stoic philosophy, they are the most important values. "If you should come across something greater than justice, honesty, self-control, courage at some time in your life," Marcus Aurelius wrote, "it must be an astonishing thing indeed." That was about two thousand years ago. Since then, we've discovered a lot of things, automobiles, the Internet, remedies for diseases that were once fatal, but have we discovered anything greater than bravery? Is there anything greater than temperance and self - restraint? Isn't it preferable to do the right thing? What could be better than the truth and comprehension? No, we haven't done so. It's improbable that we will ever do so. Every situation we encounter in life provides a chance to demonstrate these four characteristics:

1. Courage
Cowardice's polar opposite is courage. Courage isn't about getting rid of our fears, desires, or concerns; it's about behaving in the correct manner despite them.
Epictetus was once asked which phrases might aid a person's success. "Persist and resist," he continued, "should be committed to memory and obeyed." Courage is the condition of the spirit that is undisturbed by fear; self-control in the face of terror; bravery in obedience to wisdom; intrepidity in the face of death; the state that guards against accurate thinking in perilous situations; force of fortitude in the face of virtue.
"Everyone wants to know whether you've got guts. If you're brave enough?" This may have been expressed differently by the Stoics. Seneca would state that he pities those who have never been through adversity. "No one, not even you, can ever realize what you are capable of," he stated, adding, "You have gone through life without an opponent." The world wants to categorize you, which is why it will periodically throw you into unpleasant situations. Consider them not as annoyances or as tragedies, but rather as chances, as questions that need to be answered. Do I have the guts to do this? Am I a courageous person? Will I face this problem or will I try to avoid it? Will I be able to stand or will I be rolled over?
Each battle needed huge amounts of fortitude, even if it was ultimately useless. Each one necessitated defying the current quo and making one's own decision. That is Stoic bravery. Courage in the face of adversity. Face death with courage. Courage to put oneself in harm's way for the sake of others. Courage to stick to your values, even if others get away with it or are rewarded for doing so. You must have the guts to speak your views and insist on the truth.

2. Temperance
Moderation is another term for temperance. It has to do with self-control, self-discipline, and self-control. It is our capacity to prioritize long-term happiness above immediate gratification. Greed, gluttony, rapid satisfaction, addictive behavior, sloth, and procrastination are the polar opposites of this trait.

Temperance is the soul's moderation in regard to normal desires and pleasures; good discipline and harmony in regard to normal pains and pleasures; concord in regard to ruling and being ruled; ordinary personal autonomy; discipline in the spirit; rational consensus within the spirit about what is commendable and despicable; the state in which its possessor decides and is careful about what he should.

The "golden medium," as Aristotle called it, indicates that virtue is found in the center, between excess and insufficiency. Discontent and displeasure are similar with excess and demands. They're a self-destructive urge.

"Curb your desire - don't fix your heart on too many things," Epictetus said, "and you will acquire what you need." "You ask what is the correct limit to a person's wealth?" Seneca said. First, have what is necessary, and second, have what is sufficient."

Temperance is the understanding that possessing only what is necessary leads to abundance. Temperance and "self-control" were often employed interchangeably by the Stoics. Self-control, not just in the face of worldly items, but always in pleasure or agony, acclaim or disdain, failure or triumph, is essential.

3. Wisdom

Philosophy is defined as a love of wisdom. "Wisdom they describe as the knowledge of good and evil things and of what is neither good nor evil...knowledge of what we ought to select, what we need to stay aware of, and what is indifferent," Diogenes Lartius said of the Stoics in his Lives of the Eminent Philosophers.

Wisdom is the capacity to cause human happiness on its own; it is the understanding of what is good and wrong; it is the knowledge that causes happiness; it is the attitude by which we evaluate what should be done and what should not be done.

In more simple words, wisdom is the capacity to distinguish between what is good, bad, and indifferent. Good refers to behaving in a morally upright manner. Demonstrating bravery in the face of adversity, as well as temperance in the face of a desire to be greedy or engage in addictive behaviours. Bad refers to lying to get out of having to take responsibility. Choosing sloth, greed, and unhealthy habits above moderation. Disregarding justice and exploiting others or the community in order to gain an advantage. Indifferent refers to Money, possessions, celebrity, and so forth.

After gaining information, wisdom guides one's actions. "There is a gap between stimulus and response," Viktor Frankl observed. We have the capacity to pick our reaction in that area." Wisdom has an opportunity in that space. The first step is to recognize that there is a gap. That's where we either use what we've learned from our reading or chuck it out the window and behave rashly and irrationally.

Wisdom is the ability to take what a philosophy teaches and apply it in the actual world. "Works, not words," as Seneca phrased it. Virtue is good, while vice is bad, according to the Stoics. Virtue brings us closer to happiness, whereas vice drives us away from it. Wisdom is merely the capacity to recognize what is true, and by doing so, we may better direct our activities.

4. Justice

"Justice is the crowning perfection of the virtues," stated Cicero, a Roman senator and philosopher. In Stoicism, justice has a larger meaning than it does in our current legal and linguistic systems. Justice, according to the Stoics, is our obligation to our fellow man and to our community. It's the morality that guides our actions, particularly in respect to our community and people that live there. Are we polite, empathetic, respectful, honest, and generous? Do we offer assistance to those who require it? Do we contribute to our community or do we simply take?

Justice is the soul's unanimity with itself and the parts of the soul's good discipline with each other; the state that allocates to each person according to what is merited; the state on the basis of which its possessor chooses what seems to him to be just; the state that underpins a law-abiding style of living; radical egalitarianism; the state of conformity to the laws.

Marcus Aurelius deemed justice to be the most essential of the Four Stoic Virtues. "The root of all other qualities," he said. After all, how amazing is courage if it's all for one's own benefit? What value is wisdom if it isn't applied to the greater good? We must consider Cicero to comprehend the virtue of justice, who agreed with Marcus that "justice is the crowning perfection of the virtues." Cicero was regarded in his day and throughout history for more than simply a statement; he was admired for embodying those words. Because justice is your moral compass, it directs the other virtues. It helps you to direct your efforts toward the good of the entire rather than just yourself. "What is not beneficial for the beehive cannot be good for the bees," stated Marcus Aurelius. We end up harming ourselves if we harm our community. The capacity to benefit the hive, then, is justice.

- **Emotions**

A common fallacy is that a Stoic is one who tries their hardest to eliminate emotions from their life and existence, as though emotion is an awful idea to the Stoic thinker. The real rationale for the Stoics' purposeful withdrawal of emotion and passion from decision-making is not that emotions are inherently bad, but rather that rational decision-making is superior to emotional decision-making. In this aspect, the primary Stoics argue that our emotions are ultimately the result of our decisions, and that we should avoid putting the cart before the horse by utilizing emotions to motivate our decisions.

Emotions are the result of our conclusions, of believing that something good or unpleasant is occurring or is likely to occur. Many of our bad emotions are caused by erroneous judgments, yet because they are caused by our judgments, we have control over them. You may alter your emotions by altering your judgments. Despite common belief, the Stoic does not suppress or reject his emotions; rather, he does not experience them at all. This isn't as bleak as it may appear: we should overcome detrimental, negative emotions based on erroneous judgements and embrace right positive emotions, replacing rage with joy.

Stoicism believes that we can only properly feel and use our emotions if we make judgments in a logical and sensible manner, after which we can let ourselves to feel the right emotions that emerge from those decisions. As a result, rather than advocating the abolition of all feeling and desire, Stoicism educates us how to experience emotions that are more full and appropriate. The Stoics recognized the essence of emotions as much as they recognized the essence of any other sphere of human life; they simply argue that emotions must not be permitted to take prominence, so to speak, in the significantly larger cosmic system of the universal experience, at the expense of logic and reason.

- **Co-Existence in Harmony**

Stoicism also informs us that we are social creatures who must find a way to live in peace with one another in order to live a rational existence. "We were born for collaboration, like feet, like hands, like eyelids, like the rows of upper and lower teeth," So it's against nature to operate in opposition to one another, and rage or rejection is resistance." Marcus Aurelius says in his Meditations.

The Stoics also advocate living in harmony with nature. An aspect of what they imply by this is that we should recognize that we are little components of a greater, biological whole, influenced by larger forces beyond our control. Attempting to oppose these broader processes will only result in rage, disappointment, and frustration. Although there are several things we can alter in the world, there are many things we cannot, and we must recognize and accept this.

As previously said, virtue in the Stoic meaning is always a notion that must be applied to real-life events, rather than just a state of mind. This necessitates a cautious approach to topics such as environmental upkeep.

PROMISES OF STOICISM

The promises of Stoicism are divided into two for the sake of simplicity. It first teaches you how to live a happy and easy-going life called eudiamonia, and then it teaches you how to be emotionally resilient so that you may keep that happy and easy-going existence even when faced with difficulty. Let's start with the first promise and the first of the frightening words: eudaimonia.

1. Eudaimonia

The ultimate goal of life for the Stoics and all other schools of ancient thought was eudaimonia, or becoming good - *eu* with your inner *daimon* - the ideal version of oneself. The word eudaimonia is commonly translated as 'happiness,' although this does not adequately convey the philosophical meaning. It has less to do with a person's mood and more to do with the overall quality of their existence. Alternative contemporary interpretations include 'luck,' 'fulfilment,' 'blessedness,' 'well-being and, 'flourishing,' among others. It was described as follows in an old lexicon of philosophical terminology attributed to Plato but most likely authored by his immediate followers: The good constituted of all goods, perfection in terms of virtue, a capacity that suffices for living properly, among others.

Eudaimonia refers to a divine and good condition of being that mankind can aspire for and potentially achieve. A literal interpretation of eudaimonia is obtaining a condition of being comparable to a beneficent deity, or being safeguarded and cared for by one. Because this is the greatest positive condition to be in, the term is frequently translated as 'happy,' yet the divine quality of the word expands the meaning to encompass the notions of being lucky or blessed. Despite this derivation, ancient Greek ethics debates of eudaimonia are frequently performed without regard for any supernatural meaning. Nature, according to the Stoics, wants us to become the best version of ourselves. That's why the inner daimon or divine spark has been placed as a seed within each of us, so that we have the innate ability to become our best selves. In other words, it is in our nature to finish what that heavenly seed began and bring our human capacity to life. To become as near as possible to our high potential self, we must get good with our inner daimon and live in accordance with our ideal self. We need to bridge the gap between who we're capable of being and who we are right now. How are we going to do it? Areté was a term used by the Stoics to describe this. Areté, in brief, means "excellence," or "virtue," but it also has a deeper meaning: "expressing the highest version of oneself in every moment." Stoicism, as you can see, is concerned with your day-to-day behaviours and living as near to your ideal self as possible.

The Stoics' main objective was eudaimonia, or being at peace with one's inner daimon, living in accordance with one's ideal self, and expressing one's best self in every moment. But what precisely does that imply? Happiness is the most popular translation of the Greek word eudaimonia. The translations "thriving", or "flourishing" on the other hand, better convey the original sense because they imply continuous motion. You can only be nice with your daimon if your behaviours are in sync with your ideal self in the moment. You excel at living well, and you will only be pleased as a result. This prospect of eudaimonia implies that we have all we need to deal with whatever life throws at us. How else would we be able to remain cheerful even when things are difficult? Because life is relatively simple when things are going well; it only becomes tough when things appear to be working against us, when we are confronted with challenges and conflicts. This leads us to Stoicism's second promise. philosophy teaches us how to approach life's challenges with the correct mentality so that things flow smoothly.

2. Emotional or Psychological Resilience

Psychological or emotional resilience refers to our ability to handle challenging situations without being overwhelmed. We may build our resilience and equip ourselves to deal better in future hardship by practicing cognitive and behavioural skills.

As we have seen, when we talk about somebody having a "philosophical attitude" in the face of hardship, this figure of speech, which refers to emotional resilience, is most likely derived from Stoic philosophy. Stoicism's literature is primarily about coping with the types of adversity addressed in current resilience research: poverty, loss, disease, and so on. So, at first glance, the link between ancient Stoicism and current resilience-building appears to be evident.

In certain ways, Stoicism has traditionally been associated with resilience. Epictetus, the Stoic instructor, is regarded as the "patron saint of the resilient" by one modern specialist, Michael Neenan. Epictetus wonders, "But what is philosophy?" "Doesn't it imply preparing to deal with whatever comes our way?" Yes, he claims, philosophy equips us to deal with whatever comes our way. "Otherwise, it'd be like a boxer stepping out of the ring after taking a few blows." We could exit the arena with no repercussions, but if we abandoned our quest for wisdom? "So, what should each one of us say in response to each trial?" This is my expertise, and this is what I've prepared for!" A boxer will not quit the ring if he is pounded in the face; that is what he trained for, and it is his profession. A boxer will not quit the ring if he is pounded in the face; that is what he trained for, and it is his profession. The same is true for philosophers: just because life kicks, slaps, knocks, and spits us out doesn't mean we should give up and go; it simply means we should get back and keep improving. Life is like a boxing ring for us; we've joined up for punches and kicks, and this is our discipline. According to Seneca, "unharmed affluence cannot withstand a single blow," but a man who has suffered several calamities "acquires a skin calloused by suffering." This man takes the battle to the ground and continues to fight even when on his knees. He has no intention of giving up.

Stoicism helps us to develop the tools we need to handle as successfully as humanly feasible with whatever life throws our way. Whatever life throws at us, we're ready for it. We're ready to take sidekicks and hooks, never surrender, and take full advantage of it. This is Stoic philosophy's promise. Strong emotions, according to the Stoics, are our greatest weakness, especially when we allow them to govern our actions. They are poisonous to eudaimonia and the source of all human misery. Unfortunately, most of us are slaves to passions, which are powerful negative feelings such as unreasonable wrath, fear, or sadness, according to the Stoics. According to the Stoics, if desire to be capable of acting like our perfect selves, we must control our emotions and tame them so that they do not stand in the way of living a decent life.

- **Taming Limiting Emotions.**

It's critical to remember that taming limiting emotions does not entail becoming emotionless. Stoic philosophy promises a highly happy existence - eudaimonia - as well as the ability to deal successfully with any circumstances life throws at us. However, we can only deal effectively with life's obstacles if we are emotionally robust and do not allow our emotions to drag us all around. This is why, as Seneca puts it, "the glitter of gold does not dazzle our eyes more than the flash of a sword," and we can simply wave away what other people seek and dread."

The Stoics were keen observers of the human mind and possessed a wealth of psychological knowledge. They learned, for example, that it is our perception of insults that makes them harmful, not the insults themselves. They devised psychological ways to avoid and deal with bad emotions since they had a thorough grasp of our minds. Despite the fact that Stoicism is a philosophy, it has a strong psychological component. Many of its principles, such as the objective of thriving as human beings, are in line with contemporary Positive Psychology studies; this is one of the most interesting aspects of Stoicism.

Stoicism does not involve hiding or repressing one's feelings, or with being emotionless. It's more about accepting our feelings, meditating on what generates them, and learning to channel them for our own good. To put it another way, it's more about freeing ourselves from unpleasant emotions, taming rather than eradicating them. The Stoics discovered, on the other hand, that we don't have to follow our emotions' inclinations. We may teach ourselves to act calmly in the face of anger, courageously in the face of anxiety, and to travel east despite the emotion tugging us west. The objective isn't to get rid of all emotions; rather, it's to avoid becoming overwhelmed by them, despite their enormous strength. The Stoics believe that we should overcome our desires by growing stronger than them rather than by suppressing them. We will always be aware of the arising emotional wildness, but we may train ourselves to detect our proclivity to move along and then choose whether or not to do so. Stoicism will assist us in experiencing less bad emotions while also allowing us to experience more good feelings such as joy and tranquillity. It's worth noting, too, that for the Stoics, happy feelings are more of a gift than a motivation in and of themselves.

- **Tranquillity**

Stoicism is a happy philosophy of life, which may surprise you. When you read the Stoics, you'll discover happy, upbeat people who are completely appreciating everything that life has to offer. They weren't emotionless; they just realized that strong emotions were a flaw in their character that prevented them from living as fully as they might.

Remember that eudaimonia is the ultimate objective of life—the pleasant and smooth-flowing living that comes from thriving at manifesting your best version at all times. And if you are imprisoned by your emotional impulses, you will panic and act in ways that aren't even close to what you're competent of. That is the reason behind the Stoics wanting us to limit the negative consequences of powerful emotions in our life; they want us to tame the strong emotions so that we may remain in control at all times rather than allowing the emotion to take control anytime it wants. Only then will we be able to express our highest selves and, as a result, enjoy a joyful and free-flowing existence. We can portray the finest form of ourselves in every situation when we're not trapped by our emotions. There's no place for regret, anxiety, or uncertainty when we do that. The consequence is a really beneficial side effect called tranquillity.

What exactly is tranquillity? In his famous writings, Seneca discusses the power of euthymia. He explains that euthymia, which means tranquillity in Greek, is all about knowing and walking your path. It's the sensation we experience when we completely trust ourselves. You are certain that what you're doing is correct, therefore you do not need to listen to the sayings of others. You don't have to constantly doubt yourself and compare yourself to others. You have faith in what you're doing because you are giving it your all and living your principles, knowing that this is all you can do.

In today's busy world, many of us want tranquillity, the ability to remain calm, confident, and safe even in the middle of mayhem. This is precisely what we receive as a result of practicing Stoicism. It's a by-product since it's not what the Stoics were looking for to begin with. They weren't looking for tranquillity; they were looking for eudaimonia, and tranquillity was an additional benefit. So practicing Stoicism for the purpose of tranquillity would be inconsistent with the philosophy.

Tranquillity is the quiet certainty that comes from living your true self in accordance with your highest principles. Seneca claims that you get this peace of mind because you live by a constant standard, unlike the rest of humanity, who "continually ebb and flow in their decisions, floating in a situation where they alternately reject and seek things." Stoicism will provide you with several anchors to grip onto so that you may identify your path and confidently travel it. This will provide you inner peace and calm assurance at all times, even when life throws its most vicious kicks and blows at you. You know why you do what you do because you understand why you do it. You have this inner assurance that you are doing what is right, and that no matter what happens, you will stand firm like that pinnacle of strength, unaffected.

REASONS WHY YOU SHOULD STUDY STOICISM

Has it has been established previously in this book that Stoicism is widely used by quite a number of people, and some even use it unknowingly. This shows how important the principles are, giving more reasons why you should study Stoicism to allow you enjoy the full benefits of the Stoic philosophy in your life's endeavours. Stoicism has a lot to teach us, especially in these days of overabundance of passion. Furthermore, the Stoic tradition has had a greater impact on our world than you may think. The following are reasons why Stoicism is important:

- **Stoicism was designed for adversity.**

Stoicism arose in the midst of a crumbling world. Stoicism flourished at Athens just a few decades after Alexander the Great's conquests and untimely death undermined the Greece, since it provided stability and tranquillity in a period of conflict and upheaval. The Stoic philosophy did not offer monetary stability or eternal serenity, but it did promise unwavering enjoyment in this life. According to Stoicism, no enjoyment can be guaranteed if it is based on transient, ephemeral things. Our bank accounts can increase or decrease, our professions can improve or deteriorate, and even our loved ones might be snatched away from us. There is just one area that the world cannot reach: our inner selves, our decision to be bold, sensible, and good at all times.

The world may steal everything from us, but Stoicism teaches us that we all have an inner castle. "Where is the good?" said Epictetus, a Stoic philosopher who was born a slave and disabled at an early age. In the spirit of... If somebody is unhappy, remind him that he is sad only because of himself."

While it is natural to scream out in agony, the Stoic strives to be unaffected by external events, to be equally delighted in times of success and calamity. It's a difficult way of life, but the payoff is freedom from passion, the freedom from the emotions that appear to govern us when we should be controlling them. A true Stoic is not emotionless. He or she does, however, have emotional mastery, as Stoicism acknowledges that anxiety, greed, and sadness only invade our thoughts when we consciously allow them to do so.

A philosophy like Stoicism appears to be created for a tense environment, whether it's ancient Greece's tumultuous world or today's financial crisis. But, as Epictetus points out, our worlds are continually on edge as long as we try to find satisfaction in perishable things.

- **Stoicism is a leadership philosophy.**

Stoicism tells us that we must first control ourselves before we can influence circumstances. Our attempts to have an impact on the world are vulnerable to disappointment, chance, and failure, but self-control is the only type that can succeed 100 percent of the time. Leaders have discovered that a Stoic attitude gives them respect in the face of loss and protects them from arrogance in the face of success, dating back to Emperor Marcus Aurelius.

Stoicism appeals to everybody who is faced with uncertainty, which includes all of us. Leaders, on the other hand, are particularly vulnerable to danger and change, so it's no surprise that most of them find a Stoic mind-set beneficial to their psychological health. Stoicism, of course, does not ensure success. Marcus Aurelius' Meditations was one of Bill Clinton's favourite books, despite the fact that he is far from a Stoic. Cato the Younger was a firm believer in this ideology from his early manhood until his death, yet he was also prone to violent outbursts of rage, stubborn pride, and the occasional bouts of inebriation.

Cato embodied the Stoic ideal in his most daring moments, when he finally defeated Julius Caesar's army and imminent loss without blinking. The Stoics believed that we fail considerably more frequently than we succeed, and that being human means being scared, greedy, and enraged far more frequently than we'd want. They did, however, provide a practical method to be more. The more we cultivate Stoic virtues in great times, the more likely we are to locate them in ourselves when we need them the most.

- **As a Christian, You're already half-Stoic**

Think of a religion that emphasized human kinship under a beneficent creator God; that told us to mediate and control our basic urges rather than succumbing to them; that insisted, despite this, that all humans, are doomed to fail because we're human; and that spent so much time talking about "conscience" and the various aspects, or "beings," of a unitary God. All of this could ring a bell. But it was Stoicism, not Christianity, that gave birth to all of those concepts.

Christianity is a very Stoic faith, which makes sense. For centuries, Stoicism controlled Roman society, while Christianity became popular in the same civilization. Furthermore, many of the early Christian church's leaders were former Stoics. Of fact, much of Christianity's concept and language were influenced by Stoicism, because reasoning about religion throughout the first millennium required reasoning like a Stoic.

As Christianity grew in popularity, church officials began to minimize the Stoic link in order to stress the faith's distinctiveness. However, Stoicism is still present in some of the Christian religion's most fundamental terminology and principles.

- **Stoicism is made for a globalized world.**

Stoicism arose from a provincial, frequently xenophobic culture in which most people adhered to age-old distinctions of religion, nationality, and position. Stoicism is to blame if openly accepting those distinctions sounds foreign to us. Maybe the first Western philosophy to advocate global brotherhood was Aristotle's. Each of us is a citizen of our own country, but we are also "members of the vast city of gods and mankind," according to Epictetus. Marcus Aurelius, the most well-known Stoic in history, reminded himself on a daily basis to love the world as much as he loved his own city.

If the secret to pleasure is truly in our own willpower, even the greatest societal divisions become insignificant. Seneca, a Roman Stoic, lived in a society based on slavery, yet he exhorted his fellow Romans to "remember that he whom you name your slave sprung from the same stock, is looked upon by the same heavens, and lives, breathes, and dies on equal terms with yourself."

Stoicism was the appropriate philosophy for the Roman Empire, which brought an unparalleled diversity of ethnicities and religions into touch, thanks to its acceptance of cosmopolitanism, a phrase coined by Stoics that literally means "global city". Stoicism made sense in a worldwide society and continues to do so now.

- **Stoicism is the military's unofficial philosophy.**

The A-4E Skyhawk of James Stockdale was gunned down over Vietnam in 1965. "After expulsion, I had about thirty seconds to make my final comment in freedom before I landed...," he subsequently recalled. 'Five years down there, at the very least,' I said to myself. I'm leaving the realm of technology and entering Epictetus' universe.' Stockdale said that Stoicism saved his life after spending over seven years in a Vietnamese jail. Before deploying, Stockdale had spent several years studying Stoic philosophy, and he leaned on their teachings to get through his imprisonment. "Do you not know that life is a soldier's service?" Epictetus' words kept coming back to him: "...Do you realize what a terrible position you lead the army to if you ignore your duty when a serious command is given to you?" Stockdale's Stoic practice enabled him accept the awful truth of his predicament without succumbing to despair and sadness, while several of his fellow POWs tortured themselves with false expectations of an imminent release. As a war veteran who drew fortitude from Stoicism, Stockdale was not alone. Nancy Sherman, a philosophy professor at the Naval Academy, argues in her book The Stoic Warrior that Stoicism is a driving factor behind the military attitude, particularly in its focus on perseverance, inner strength, and self-control. "Many soldiers and students felt they had returned home," Sherman says, when her philosophy lecture at Annapolis came to the Stoic thinkers.

2
THE PILLARS OF STOICISM

The dual concept that ethics is vital to the endeavour, and that the study of ethics is to be supported by two other disciplines of investigation, what the Stoics termed "logic" and "physics," is a basic component of Stoic philosophy. These come together to create the three pillars of Stoicism.

We'll look at each pillar in turn, but first it's vital to understand why and how they're related. Stoicism was a practical philosophy whose main objective was to assist individuals in leading eudaimonic lives, which the Stoics defined as lives spent practicing the Stoic virtues, also known as the Cardinal virtues. Later in the Roman era, the emphasis switched to achieving apatheia, However, the practice of the concepts of ethics made this conceivable as well.

This was to be backed by the study of the other two concepts, "logic," which was more comprehensive than the advanced technological meaning of the term, including not only logic sensu stricto but also a theory of knowledge, as well as psychological science, and "physics," which the Stoics defined as roughly a combination of metaphysics and natural science - the former including theology. Thus, "logic" roughly refers to the study of how to think about the world, whereas "physics" refers to the study of the world itself.

Because Stoicism is a purely naturalistic philosophy, Logic and Physics are linked to Ethics. Even when the Stoics allude to God or soul, they are addressing physical entities that are associated with the rational principle ingrained in the world and whatever makes human reason possible, respectively. To demonstrate the link between Physics, Logic, and Ethics, Stoics frequently used artistic imagery. Some academics, for example, organize these features of Stoicism in the shape of an egg. The yolk denotes physics, the white is ethics, and the shell denotes logic. According to these researchers, physics lies at the heart of Stoicism since ethics are impossible to discern without understanding the workings of the cosmos. The firmness of logic, in contrast to the flexibility of ethics, produces the shell. The three pillars of Stoicism will be discussed based on this Stoic egg. However, before going into detail about each facet of Stoic philosophy, it's crucial to note that they are all interconnected, and without one, the system will fall apart.

1. Stoic Logic

We may take for granted our rational reasoning about cause and consequence, but human thought hasn't always worked that way. And, let's face it, there are still a lot of individuals today who cannot think of logical reasoning and are completely guided by their emotions. Logic is a skill. The Stoics' wise men were adept at philosophical argument. One of the remaining sources for Stoic logic is Diogenes Laertius, who wrote: "And because of this, the Stoics may say that the wise man is always a dialectician in logical things. For everything is perceived through the lens of debate: both what belongs to the field of physics and what belongs to the field of ethics."

Propositional logic is a Stoic method of logic that was given by Diodorus Cronus, one of Zeno's early instructors. Propositional logic, also known as logos as the Stoics called it, is a method of approaching logical reasoning through assertions or propositions. This sets it apart from prior logic schools, such as Aristotle's term-based logic. Chrysippus, a Stoic from the post-Zeno era, expanded on this technique of propositional thought and established the Syllogistic deductive reasoning approach.

What is propositional logic, and how does it work? Let's take a closer look at the concept: To begin with, a proposition is a phrase that is either true or untrue.

Here's an example. Take a glance out the window if you're watching this video during the day. Outside, it is most likely bright. As a result, you may make the following claim: "it is light." This statement is correct if it is truly daylight. However, this assertion is incorrect in the middle of the night. To clarify this, we may create the following statement to add a little more complexity to the argument: "It is bright if it is day." This system of reason, according to the Stoics, is what regulates our reality. This is referred to as Logos. As a result, the term logic has become extensively used over the world to denote the principles of existence.

Many current applications rely on propositional logic, which is more than just a relic of Greek philosophy. Stoic logos concepts are being used today in fields like computer circuit design. When it comes to a topic like logic, it's easy to fall into the trap of thinking about it in terms of popular views, and to confuse the Stoic idea of logic thought with those popular beliefs. However, there is a crucial distinction to be made between the two. Everything in the cosmos is ordered by divine logic, according to Stoic theory, but the popular understanding of logic is more closely tied to what Stoic philosophers refer to as "rational mind." Rationality, or logical thought, is the Stoic's attitude to life and decision-making, which is devoid of emotional and excessive passion limitations. This method allows the Stoic to make judgments based on the most important concerns in each scenario while also reaching the most effective anticipated outcome based on rational analysis. To simplify your early knowledge and practice of propositional logic, it is recommended that you begin by looking at the fundamental propositions, or premises, that are widely used as the foundation for certain popular arguments. You'll notice that a lot of what appear to be complicated arguments and methods of thinking are actually built on a sequence of very fundamental and basic principles. You could also notice how many popular current arguments and claims are built on erroneous assumptions, making the final conclusion obtained from such defective propositions untrustworthy. You should make it a goal to constantly make sure that your own arguments are based on sound and logical assumptions, guaranteeing that your conclusions and final claims are rock solid and credible.

Mastering logical problems, studying paradoxes, and dissecting arguments were all part of logic training. However, it was not meant to be an aim in itself; rather, it was meant to help the Stoics develop their reasoning faculties. As a result, Stoic logic was a tool of self-discovery. Its goal was to encourage ethical introspection, secure and confident argumentation, and bring the student to the truth. The ultimate outcome would be a consistent, clear, and exact idea that reveals uncertainty, murkiness, and irregularity. Diogenes Lartius presents a list of dialectical qualities, which Chrysippus most likely invented.

2. Stoic Physics

What we now call natural science, theology, and metaphysics are all included in the Stoic concept of Physics. In terms of natural science and cosmology, remember that the Stoics wanted to "live according to nature," which necessitates our best efforts to comprehend nature. This also suggests a completely different perspective on natural science than the present one: its study is secondary to helping us live a eudaimonic lifestyle.

The cosmos, according to Stoic Philosophy, is a material, thinking substance called "God" or simply Nature. This quickly elucidates the significant difference between Stoicism and other types of Hellenistic Philosophies coming from the early Greek age, which mostly avoided the concept of a single deity. However, it is important to note that Stoic Philosophy does not imply believing in a loving, Abrahamic-style God who rules over a cosmos he created. Stoic philosophy, on the other hand, teaches that the Universe is God and that all occurrences are ruled by fate, which the Stoics refer to as the Universe's logic. This gives Stoics desire to live in harmony with reason, or natural logic. Living in harmony with nature necessitates a thorough awareness of the natural world. Because we can't properly relate the Stoic understanding of physics to our current metaphysics, it's better to call it nature. Stoic physics is, in a nutshell, their interpretation of the cosmos. Stoic physics, like ethics, is a large system of concept and ideas.

As established earlier, Stoics believed in Logos, a Godlike being who was the all-encompassing power of reason. Existence, in their opinion, is founded on pneuma and matter. Matter is all we can experience with our senses, yet it is also inert and lifeless on its own, as well as destructible. The active energy driving the universe' ever-changing expression is pneuma, which is entirely mixed with passive matter and therefore cannot be annihilated, according to the Stoics. Pneuma, according to Chrysippus, is the carrier of Logos that constructs matter. Simply defined, pneuma is what brings the cosmos to life. The existence of life, the movement of stars and planets, and the waves of the sea are all pushed by pneuma and founded on the logical principle of Logos.

According to Stoic philosophy, the above processes are responsible for the universe's ongoing alternating production and destruction in a never-ending cycle known as palingenesis. The Stoics formed the belief that the human soul is an everlasting aspect of the universe's existence and process as a result of this concept. This concept of the soul's ultimate immortality is, of course, completely compatible with most current religions.

Everything is predetermined, according to the Stoics. They also contended that, depending on our decisions, there are a plethora of alternative realities to choose from, and hence a plethora of possible pathways to take. This soft-determinism resembles Islamic and Christian beliefs in that our fates are inscribed in the stars on one hand, but we still have free will on the other.

3. Stoic Ethics

Stoic Ethics was more than a theoretical subject; it was a very practical one. Indeed, ethics— known as the study of how to conduct one's life—was the aim of practicing philosophy, especially for the later Stoics. "The philosopher's lecture room is a hospital: you ought not to walk out of it in a state of pleasure, but in pain—for you are not in good health when you come!" Epictetus famously stated. Epictetus' starting point was the famous control dilemma, as stated at the opening of the Enchiridion: "We are accountable for certain things, but we cannot be held responsible for others."

Stoics are sometimes misinterpreted because the language they used referred to notions that were not the same as those used now. Because Stoic ethics emphasized independence from "passion" through following "reason," the word "stoic" has come to denote unemotional or insensitive to pain. The Stoics did not strive to suppress emotions; rather, they tried to change them via a firm "asksis," which allows one to gain clear judgment and internal tranquillity. Temperance is divided into discipline, self-control, and modesty, with logic, contemplation, and attention as techniques of self-discipline. The core of Stoic ethics, which it borrowed from the Cynics, is that good consists in the state of the soul itself; in knowledge and self-control. The precept of Stoic ethics was to "follow where reason leads."

Stoic ethics emphasizes that following "reason" leads to liberation from "passion." The contemporary concept of a "stoic" person is derived from this, with a "stoic" person being someone who is extremely logical and not prone to showing strong emotions. This is regrettable, because the original notion of Stoic Philosophy was not that emotion had no place in human experience, but rather that reason is the logic of creation, and that we should live by it.

The Stoics claim that we may establish our ethics once we have mastered the skill of reason. They made a distinction between virtue and vice. Virtue was split into four categories by the Stoics, which includes courage, moderation, justice, and wisdom. They classified vice into cowardice, injustice, intemperance, and folly in the same way.

There's a large grey space between vice and virtue where things aren't either harmful or nice. The Stoics refer to this group as "indifferents." Whether or not you engage in these indifferents in a moral manner depends on the circumstances, and, once again, your ability to reason aids you in making decisions. To put it another way, indifferents are not always dangerous or beneficial; it all depends on how you utilize them.

Any current version of ethics that refuses to, at least in part, depend on core Stoic precepts in its statements about what is ethically acceptable against what is not would be difficult, if not impossible, to discover. As a result, we should at least have a rudimentary comprehension of the foundations of Stoic Philosophy in the domain of ethical behaviour of human.

3
STOICISM IN THE MODERN WORLD

STOICISM IN THE WORLD TODAY

Stoicism has found a place in our modern way of thinking, not only in novels and movies, but also in the statement of a "responsibility towards God and Country," as we've seen in previous chapters. We can perceive Stoicism as a significant force in current politics if we analyse the fields of actual influence of Stoicism on our modern civilization more closely.

We can also see the effect of Roman Stoicism and its goal to bring rule and order to the rest of the globe in today's continuous globalization process. This is eerily similar to the approach taken by the United States in recent years, in which it has sought to "liberate" specific Middle Eastern countries from dictatorial regimes. It's reasonable to say that in the twenty-first century, a Stoic style to leadership is better to a more emotive approach, especially when the unlikely-but-possible prospect of a Nuclear Third World War is considered. Stoicism emphasizes that we must first master our impulses and inner desires before we can have any effect on the world around us. Stoicism has had a major influence on our present renaissance, and it is worth noting that the first declaration of human rights was produced by individuals who were heavily influenced by Stoicism.

Since the early periods of emperor Marcus Aurelius, international leaders have discovered that adopting a Stoic mind-set is always the safest choice when it comes to concerns of state, as it ensures the least amount of shame in the case of failure, while avoiding tremendous arrogance in the event of triumph. These factors have greatly influenced the appeal of a Stoic approach in contemporary world leaders' judgments and actions.

Stoicism has made its way into entertainment media in addition to its effect on modern politics. The dispassionate and extremely rational character "Spock" from the massively popular "Star Trek" series, which is clearly based on Stoicism, is a notable illustration of this.

It's fair to say that philosophy is undergoing a modern-day renaissance, as its relevance and use in real-life circumstances grow increasingly evident and popular. In our current environment, when everything appears to be rushed and pressed, it's easy to see how the Stoic approach to reasonable and level-headed thinking may be beneficial. Stoicism has definitely been accepted as one of the leading Philosophies of choice in twenty - first - century pop culture, as seen by the explosion of online Stoic websites. The originators of this Hellenistic school of thought wanted Stoicism to be a way of life, not just an intellectual exercise, and this great public appeal of Stoicism today is in accordance with their original vision. As previously established, Zeno of Citium was a major advocate of applying Stoic philosophy to practical problems. Marcus Aurelius' Meditations are yet another example of an early Stoic thinker applying philosophy to all aspects of his life.

Stoicism has become ideology for Heads of State and also writers of Hollywood scripts and literature, therefore it is not an exaggeration to say that it is one of the cornerstones of our modern civilization. Anyone concerned in understanding the dynamics of the twenty-first century should have at least a fundamental understanding of Stoic philosophy and ideas. You may get bewildered by the judgment process of people in charge if you lack this fundamental understanding, but you may experience feelings of fear and worry rather than insight into everyday happenings and global decisions.

You may be pleased with the fundamental understanding and insight offered by your introductory study of Stoic Philosophy, or you may desire to continue your research of this school of thought. This practice can be done in a variety of ways, as practically all colleges and universities offer Stoic Philosophy courses. If this alternative is too costly or impracticable, you can look into the possibilities of finding decent books on the subject to read. Understand that this is how Zeno, the originator of Stoic ideas, became interested in the study of philosophy in general.

Always recall that it is preferable to have a broad grasp of Stoic ideas and then put at least a few of them into practice than to just consume as much information as possible on the topic without ever incorporating it into your everyday life. You could perhaps try to cultivate the habit of viewing the modern society through the educated eyes of a Stoic sage, gaining insight into the hidden reasons for the complexities at work in the world, and developing an admiration for the logical and rational dynamics of the cosmic universe that we all call home.

WHY STOICISM IS IMPORTANT IN TODAY'S WORLD

Stoicism is still relevant today because of its ageless and simple philosophy. Its proponents created and spread it in such a way that individuals from all millennia and socioeconomic classes might benefit from it. The following factors contribute to Stoicism's importance in our world today:

- **Attractive and Practical Approach**: The Stoics' teachings were straightforward and simple to understand. Even today, everyone with a little effort may learn and apply their lessons to their everyday lives. Despite the fact that some of the original masters never wrote a single word for the historical evidence and that some of their original manuscripts were lost or destroyed, the followers of those Stoic preachers took great care to capture their teachings in books that we may read today.

- **Philosophy for the People:** The traditional Stoic instructors taught in such a way that even the most common of the ordinary people could listen in. They preached in public locations and authored publications that anybody may freely copy, quote, and disseminate. They were unconcerned about attributions or copyright issues. As a result, the majority of their sermons were widely printed, cited, and disseminated. And they're still readily available for anyone who wants to study and practice it.

- **Modern Cognitive Research Backs Stoicism's Key Ideas:** Modern cognitive science backs up some of Stoicism's core beliefs. A Stoic tenet proved to be a powerful antidote to anxiety and sadness. In fact, it paved the way for counselling techniques like CBT, which asserts that our negative thoughts, feelings, and actions create problems, and REBT, which says our thoughts about happenings leads to behavioural and emotional.

- **Free to All:** The key Stoicism works written by ancient authors have always been free to read. In an internet-powered world with selfless repositories like Project Gutenberg, this is especially true. Stoicism was conceived as a philosophy for the masses, and it remains so till this day.

STOICISM'S RELEVANCE IN MODERN TIMES

Stoicism is still important today because it helps modern women and men organize their lives. Today, a practicing Stoic is seen as a calm, contented someone who is frequently sought out for wise guidance and sincere advice. People are still inspired by ancient philosophy to rethink and reorganize their life in order to seek eudemonia.

In today's entrepreneurial environment, successes and failures coexist. One of these cannot exist without the other in any firm, whether it is a small start-up or a large enterprise. And any business owner, at any level, may become engrossed in the emotions that come with success or failure, as well as the need to stay relevant.

Stoicism has recently resurfaced among major and small company owners seeking to align their thinking with the practical components of the ancient philosophy. So they could deal calmly with their hectic and frequently unpredictable existence.

The Stoics have a favourable impact on others around them, contributing to a less selfish and more peaceful world. Stoicism aims to imbue us with two qualities: joy and potential. It resembles happiness science in certain ways. If we think about it, joy and potential are indeed the two things that everyone strives for in life. The ultimate goal of human life, according to Stoicism, is to reflect back on a virtuous life after one dies. To have a good life, one must be wise and live in harmony with nature.

STOICISM AND CHRISTIANITY

It should be obvious from the start that Stoicism, in its purest form as taught by Zeno as well as other Hellenistic philosophers, is incompatible with Christianity. The ancient Stoic concept that the Universe is God cannot be reconciled with Christian conviction that a beneficent God who created the Universe retains authority over it as a Divine Ruler. However, we must credit Stoicism with being the first school of thought — prior to the lives and times of Jesus Christ — to move away from the fatalistic attitude that nothing truly matters. Early Stoics also drifted away from the concept of several gods and toward monotheistic, or belief in a deity, which is obviously in line with Christian beliefs. Besides the points of resemblance between early Stoicism and Christianity mentioned above, there are schools of subsequent Stoic Philosophy that are clearly completely compliant with Christianity in their entirety, such as the Philosophy of the Roman Stoics, who believed that every Roman had a "duty towards God and Country." Another point of convergence between Stoicism and Christianity is the requirement that we obey God's Will rather than mindlessly following our own selfish wants. Despite the fact that the Roman Stoics do not always precisely name the deity they worship, their desire to serve the Will of a force greater than themselves is shared by Christians. Some philosophers may claim that Christianity acquired some of its concepts from Stoic thinking, while Christian academics will contend that the Bible is the basis of all Christian religion. It is most correct to say that Stoic Philosophy evolved to the point where it was compatible with traditional Christianity. In the end, however, there are significant distinctions between Stoic thought and Christian faith.

AFTERWORD

The teachings of Stoicism have been proven to be beneficial to those who practiced it and their environment. In order for you adopt this philosophy for your good, the, following are the activities you must carry out to get you to started on your journey to Stoicism.

- **Keep records**

The slave Epictetus. Emperor Marcus Aurelius. Seneca, the dramatist and power broker. These three wildly disparate guys lived wildly disparate lives. They did, however, appear to have one habit in common, which is Keeping records.

Keeping records is more than just a basic diary in Stoicism. The philosophy is everyday practice. I'm getting ready for the day ahead. I'm pondering the events of the day. Reminding ourselves of the lessons we've learnt through our instructors, books, and life experiences. It is not enough to merely hear these lessons once; rather, one must practice them again, mull them over in their minds, and, most essentially, write them down while feeling them flow through their fingers.

Stoicism is meant to be practiced and followed on a regular basis. It's not a philosophy that you read once and instantly comprehend on a soul level. No, it's a lifetime endeavor that takes effort, repetition, and focus. It's putting something up for you to evaluate, have on hand, and completely comprehend. In no way, shape, or form. Not just at once. But on a daily basis over the period of a year, preferably year after year. And, if Epictetus is correct, it's something you should have on hand at all times, which is why a daily playlist of the greatest songs appealed to us so much. Keeping records is Stoicism in this sense. Having one without the other is nearly impossible.

- **The control dichotomy**

Making a distinction between what we can alter and what we cannot is the most fundamental discipline in Stoic philosophy. What we have control over and what we don't have control over. When a flight is delayed due to bad weather, ranting at an airline employee won't help. There's no way to make yourself taller or shorter or to be born in a foreign nation by wishing. You can't make someone who looks like you, no matter how hard you try. Furthermore, time spent flinging oneself at immovable objects is time wasted away from the things we can influence.

You will not only be happy, but you will have a great edge over other individuals who fail to see they are waging an unwinnable struggle if you can focus on making clear what aspects of your day are within your control and what parts are not.

- **Control your perceptions**

The Stoics developed a practice known as "Spinning the Barriers Upside Down." They were attempting to make it hard to avoid practicing philosophy. Because every "bad" becomes a fresh source of good if you can appropriately turn a situation upside down. Assume for a moment that you are attempting to assist somebody and that they are irritable or unwilling to comply. The practice claims that rather than making your life much harder, they are steering you toward new qualities, such as understanding and patience. Alternatively, the loss of anyone close to you; an opportunity to demonstrate fortitude.
To a devout Stoic, there is no good or wrong. Only perception exists. You have complete power over how you perceive things. You have the option of extrapolating beyond your first perception. If you make dispassion your initial response, you'll see that everything becomes an opportunity.

- **Practice with Bad Situations.**

Seneca, who was well-off as Nero's counsel, proposed that we set aside a specific number of days every month to exercise poverty. Take little food, put on your worst clothing, and leave your house and bed behind. When you're confronted with want, he says, you'll wonder, "Is this what I used to fear?"
It's critical to keep in mind that this is an exercise, not a figure of speech. He doesn't mean "consider" hardship; he means "experience" it. Because you're always scared that someone or something will take it away, comfort is the worst form of servitude. However, if you can not only predict but also rehearse disaster, chance loses its power to derail your plans.
Anxiety and terror are emotions that are rooted on uncertainty rather than experience. Anyone who has ever placed a large wager on themselves understands how much effort both states require. The solution is to address the issue of ignorance. Make yourself acquainted with the things you are terrified of, the worst-case situations. Practice what you're afraid of, whether it's in your head or in real life. The disadvantage is nearly usually temporary or reversible.

- **Be empathetic in your viewpoint**

This activity isn't only about seeing how insignificant we are in the great scheme of things. The second, subtler point is to tap into what the Stoics refer to as sympatheia, or a sense of reciprocal interconnectedness with all mankind. "In outer space, you get an immediate global awareness, a people orientation, an overwhelming discontent with the status of the world, and a need to do something about it," said astronaut Edgar Mitchell, one of the first individuals to really see a true view from above. Remind yourself of your responsibility to others by taking a step back from your own problems.

- **Know that all is temporary**

It's vital to notice that the term 'emotion' is not used in the current sense of being enthusiastic or caring about something. When the Stoics talk about conquering 'emotions,' which they termed patheiai, they're talking about unreasonable, unhealthy, and excessive impulses and emotions, as Don Robertson describes in his book. Anger is an excellent example. What's vital to remember is that, instead of excessive pleasure, they strive to replace them with eupatheiai, such as joy.
Returning to the exercise's premise, it's as easy as remembering how little you are. Also, keep in mind how insignificant most things are. Keep in mind that accomplishments might be temporary, and that you only have them for a short time. Why does it matter if everything is temporary? What mattered, and what was vital to the Stoics, was being a good person and doing the right thing right now.

- **Don't keep your expectations high at all times**

The premeditatio malorum, interpreted as pre-meditation of evils, is a Stoic activity in which we imagine what may go wrong or be taken away from us. It assists us in anticipating life's inevitable disappointments. Even when we have earned something, we don't always get it. Everything isn't as simple and easy as we believe it is. We must psychologically prepare ourselves for this to occur. It's one of the Stoics' most effective exercises for increasing resilience and strength.
Seneca, for example, would begin by going over or rehearsing his intentions, such as going on a vacation. Then, in his thoughts, he would go over the things that may go wrong or prevent it from happening: a storm, the captain falling ill, the ship being attacked by pirates. He wrote to a friend, "Nothing happens to the wise man contrary to his expectations." "...nor do all things turn out for him as he wishes, but as he reckons—and above all, he reckons that something will thwart his ambitions." Seneca was always prepared for disturbance and worked that disruption into his plans as a result of this practice. He was built for either failure or success.

- **Love Fate**

Friedrich Nietzsche, the renowned German philosopher, described his formula for human greatness as amor fati, or love of fate. "That one does not want anything to be different, not in the future, not in the past, not for life. Not just suffer, much less conceal, what is essential, but cherish it."
This attitude was not only common to the Stoics, but it was also something they welcomed. "A roaring fire produces flame and light out of everything that is tossed into it," Emperor Marcus Aurelius wrote two thousand years ago in his personal notebook, which would become known as Meditations. "Do not look for things to happen the way you want them to; rather, desire for what occurs to happen the way it happens: then you will be happy," Epictetus, a crippled slave who has suffered adversity after adversity, said.
This is why amor fati is a Stoic practice and philosophy for getting the best of whatever life throws at you: treating every moment, no matter how difficult, as something to be accepted rather than avoided. To not just accept it, but to cherish it and grow as a result of it. Obstacles and difficulty, like air to a flame, create fuel for your ability.

- **Meditate on your death**

Memento Mori—the ancient habit of reflecting on mortality that dates back to Socrates, who declared that the true practice of philosophy is "about nothing else except dying and being dead". "You may abandon life right now," Marcus Aurelius wrote in his Meditations. Let that guide your actions, words, and thoughts." That served as a personal reminder to keep living a virtue-filled life right now, rather than waiting.

If you miss the point, contemplating your mortality is merely sad. This idea is both energizing and humbling to the Stoics. One of Seneca's biographies is titled Dying Every Day, which is hardly unexpected. After all, it was Seneca who advised us to tell ourselves before going to bed, "You may not wake up tomorrow," and "You may not sleep again," as reminders of our mortality. "Keep death and exile before your eyes each day, together with everything that appears horrible," Epictetus advised his students. "By doing so, you'll never have a base idea nor an excessive desire." Utilize those lessons and dwell on them on a regular basis to help you live your life as best and not waste a single second.

ACHIEVING HAPPINESS WITH STOICISM

A lot has been said about Stoicism in previous parts of this book, and it has been emphasized that the core characteristics of the philosophy is to help people live their best lives, while being good, with virtues, self-control, and happiness. In this section, the core principles of Stoicism that brings happiness to the life of an individual will be discussed and explained. This principle includes Eudaimonia, taking responsibility, living with Virtues, and Focusing on what you can control. Each of these principles have been discussed in previous parts of this book, but further explanations will be done in this section on how they bring happiness to the lives of individuals.

- **Eudaimonia**

At the heart of the Stoic principles of happiness lies eudaimonia, the ultimate goal of life agreed upon by all ancient philosophies. This is the basic promise of Stoic philosophy, and it is about living a supremely joyful and smoothly running existence. It is all about living our best life. That's pretty much what we all want. To prosper and live happy lives. It's for this reason that it's at the heart of the Stoic Happiness principles. The word's Greek origins entails getting along - *eu* with your inner *daimon*, your ultimate self. And that can be done by embracing virtues.

- **Focus on what you can control**

This is Stoicism's most important premise. At all times, we must concentrate on the things we can control and accept the rest as it comes. What is already in place must be accepted since undoing it is beyond our ability. What is beyond our control is ultimately irrelevant to our well-being. What matters for our growth is whatever we decide to do with the external conditions we are given. So, no matter what scenario we find ourselves in, we can always attempt to make the best of it and live in accordance with our best self.

- **Take on Responsibilities**

You are the solitary source of both good and bad. This follows other principles, which state that external goods do not important for a happy existence, and that cultivating qualities, which are under your control, is sufficient for success. Furthermore, you are accountable for your life since every external incident over which you have no control provides an area over which you do have influence, namely how you respond to the experience. This is fundamental in Stoicism; it is our perception of circumstances that determines whether we are happy or unhappy. When you resolve to give external circumstances no more control over you, you may build a tower of strength.
Stoicism emphasizes that we are solely responsible for our own pleasure and misery. It also teaches that accepting this duty will help us achieve eudaimonia. On the other side, the victim mentality, which is blaming external events for our unhappiness, will make living a happy life an unattainable aim to achieve.

- **Live with Virtues**

In every moment, present your finest self. We need to narrow the gap between what we are capable of and what we're really doing if we are to be on good terms with our highest selves. It's all about becoming the best version of yourself right now. It's about acting rationally and living in accordance with our deepest ideals. This is certainly easier than it sounds, but separating good from evil and focusing on what we can control can help us achieve this lofty aim.

Living a life of virtue entails expressing what you're capable of right now. It entails being your ultimate self, getting along with your inner daimon, and obtaining eudaimonia, which is defined as a pleasant and perfectly flowing life.

Consider virtue to be a type of knowledge or strength that enables you to do the right thing at all times so that your actions are in keeping with your best self, for instance, being disciplined, courageous, and compassionate. Virtue is about striving to be the best version of yourself at all times. And if you can accomplish that, you'll have a positive relationship with your higher self and live a pleasant, easy-going existence. If you're lacking at expressing your best self, regret and worry will creep out of the shadows and spread sorrow.

THE STOIC PERSONALITY TRAITS

Generally, being stoic is often regarded as a positive quality. A stoic disposition makes a person more effective in their activities, less persuaded by little changes in their lifestyle, and far more difficult to emotionally harm. They are realistic and, as a result of their capacity to persevere in the face of adversity, attain their objectives with greater ease than others.

The following are statements that best describe the personality traits of a Stoic, or characters that perfectly show that a person is Stoic:

- They operate based on reason rather than emotion.
- They concentrate on what they can control and ignore what they can't.
- They gladly accept their situation and attempt to make the best of it.
- They remain calm and assured, regardless of what you throw at them.
- They are grateful for what they have and never grumble.
- They are quiet and unattached to the outside world.
- Practical wisdom, justice, kindness, courage, and self-discipline are among their qualities.
- They treat people with kindness, generosity, and forgiveness.
- They live in peace with each other, with people, and with nature.
- Their decisions are well-considered, and they accept full responsibility.
- Setbacks do not deter them.
- They are quick to adjust to new situations.
- They always learn from their errors.
- They are devoted to finding solutions.

SOME STOIC EXERCISES FOR SELF-IMPROVEMENTS

We have gone through detailed explanations on the concept of Stoicism and other various concepts that are associated with it, including the pillars of Stoicism, and common Stoic practices. It is also very important for us to give detailed expositions to the practical Stoic exercises a person can engage in for self-improvements. As a matter of facts, this section appears as the practical part of this book, which explains how you can actually apply all the concepts and principles you have learnt in your day-to-day interactions and activities.

Therefore, to further enhance your learning, some practical stoic exercises for self-improvements are explained below:

- **Remind Yourself That Everything Is Ephemeral**

Consider your own mortality for a moment. Life on Earth is finite; it is a loan that you don't know when you'll have to repay. Make the most of it and keep in mind that "you and your loved ones are mortal."

Things are not genuinely yours. It's possible that your automobile will be taken. Hair and even your body might be lost. Don't become too connected to things; they won't matter in the end. Life is actually ephemeral, and the ones we love can be taken from us unexpectedly and without warning. You're also a mortal being. You might not be alive to see tomorrow.

Remind yourself how valuable life is right now, and how valuable your loved ones are, because they may not be with you much longer. Appreciate what you have and keep in mind that everything is temporary.

- **Always Practice Virtue**

It is best practice to ask yourself the best approaches to make use of at any point in time, when confronted with challenging or confusing situations. It is also important to ask yourself how best you can make use of virtue and reason at every point in time.

You may utilize any situation, any hardship, as an opportunity to practice virtue and grow as a person. All you have to do is apply reason and virtue on a regular basis. With anything that happens, you may cultivate virtue. That's the bare minimum you can do. That's a simple approach to accept anything that happens gracefully since you can learn something from it, such as how to practice virtue.

- **Practice The Situation You're Most Afraid Of**

For a short while, deprive yourself of something. For example, six months without purchasing new clothing, one week without hot baths, three days without morning tea, and so on. Then, when you do those stuffs again, relish them to the fullest.

Things are taken for granted by us. You will enjoy those things much more afterwards if you choose to go without them for a few days.

There are three parts to the concept. Firstly, it helps us to be more appreciative of our lives and not take things for granted. Secondly, it helps us to be unconcerned about losing everything. Thirdly, it helps us seek for balance. To Be freer by owning less.

- **Listen More and Talk Less**

In talks, pay attention to yourself and others. You will notice how everyone is attempting to link what is being stated to themselves. Don't talk too much; instead, strive to listen and help others.

The Stoic's best friend is silence. Partaking in gossip and condemning individuals who are not even there is just not a noble thing to do. Also, don't be too emphatic in talking about yourself. Everybody talks largely about themselves, thus you would better listen and be of service rather than chatting about yourself alone.

- **Examine Your First Impressions and Consider Your Options Before Acting.**

Put your initial impressions to the test. Choose a more intelligent answer if they are unhelpful. It's possible that you won't need to react at all. We have a tendency to respond to minor things. This isn't required, and we can eliminate it.

The majority of the time, nothing truly dreadful has occurred. So relax, take a big breath, and avoid the need to retaliate right away.

It is of no use to get worked up over something we cannot change. It is just our reaction that we have control over. So pick the best response you can and move on. In many circumstances, the wisest response is to do nothing.

- **Consider The Worst-Case Scenario**

Think of your plans for the next several days, consider what may go wrong and come up with a clever answer. Question yourself about the worst that may happen, before you do something. That's basic Stoicism, and it's one of its central ideas to be ready for the worst and still be able to handle it calmly and pick the best course of action.

Many individuals have some type of plan, and when something goes wrong, they suffer an emotional breakdown. This is no longer helpful and may be avoided. If you can visualize an unpleasant circumstance before it occurs, you will be able to cope better and remain calmer, allowing you to make the best of it. You'll be upset only if you didn't see it coming.

- **Include A "Reserve Clause" In Your Actions.**

What is something you want to undertake but aren't sure how it will turn out? Use the reserve clause to protect yourself. Tell your family, "See you later if fate allows," after you leave the house. She won't be pleased, but it's good practice for you.

Only our own ideas and actions are under our control. We have no direct influence over anything else. This is why the Stoics frequently included a reserve clause in their deeds. For example, you set a goal for yourself and work hard to attain it. However, because somethings are beyond your control, you add a reserve clause to the action, such as "fate permitting," ,"if nothing prevents me," or "God willing." This necessitates giving your all for everything that is under your control, and then accepting anything happens that is beyond your control. You understand that the final result is beyond your control.

- **Forgive Others' Mistakes**

Tell yourself that the perpetrator didn't know any better before you become furious. But you do, and as a result, you are able to be compassionate and forgiving. When someone wrongs you, don't seek vengeance, as being cruel is a sign of weakness. Instead, choose to be patient and compassionate. Instead of blaming wrongdoers, feel sorry for them since they are blinded by their intellect. If someone is cruel to you, try to consider it as a learning experience. Scratches come while we're all learning and attempting to improve. So forget about it and go on.
Everyone attempts to do what he feels is right, according to the Stoics. Even though it's clear that it isn't.

- **Love Your Fate (Amor Fati)**

Whenever there is any kind of occurrence, ask yourself whether there is anything you can do about it. Accept things as it is if it isn't within your control but rather under fate's. There's no use in battling with reality, it'll simply make you sad. It is detrimental to not want reality to be anything other than it is. Ensure that you embrace circumstances as they are and as they come rather than trying to pass judgment on them.
The Stoics attempted to concentrate on what they could control. And one of them wasn't fate. As a result, they counselled accepting and loving reality as it is rather than wishing for it to be otherwise. Resenting what happened is a mistaken assumption that you have a choice in the situation.

- **Appreciate Your Blessings**

Consider how badly you would desire the things you have if you didn't. Note down three things you are thankful for, for example. This is done by avoiding buying items you don't need, enjoying what you already have, and not becoming overly connected to what you are grateful for.
The Stoics practiced minimalism. They decided to cherish and be appreciative of what they had rather than yearn for what they lacked.

- **Consider Yourself to Be Dead**

You died the night before and have been given a second chance on this planet. Make two separate lists with answers to these questions: First, what do you consider to be the most significant aspects of your life? Second, what are you truly doing with your time?
Compare the lists and decide on one issue to improve in the next days.

This can also be construed in various ways. It might be a terrible mental image of the worst-case scenario, which is death. It might imply forgetting about the past and focusing solely on the present. Don't be concerned with the past; instead, focus on the present. You only have today. It will benefit you to take full advantage of it and make the most of it. It is an excellent tool for avoiding haphazard decisions and acts. It allows you to concentrate on what is genuinely essential. So you don't waste time on frills and focus on the important things.

- **Evaluate Your Day**

Commit to doing decent, better, and best reflection. Each night, before you go to bed, ask yourself these three questions. What have you accomplished today? What do you think you can improve on? And how could you improve on yourself to do better? This activity alone can be quite beneficial to your personal growth.

This is beneficial since you need to review the things you performed well previously. This is a great way to motivate yourself and improve your positive muscles.

www.ingramcontent.com/pod-product-compliance
Lightning Source LLC
Chambersburg PA
CBHW081126080526
44587CB00021B/3761